M000079083

upside
∪ʍop

D E V O T I O N

EXTREME ACTION FOR A REMARKABLE GOD

Other books in the
"Upside-Down" Series

Upside-Down Leadership: Rethinking Influence and Success

Upside-Down Freedom: Inverted Principles for Christian Living

Upside-Down Results: God Tags People for His Purposes

upside uʍop

D E V O T I O N

EXTREME ACTION FOR A REMARKABLE GOD

taylor field

NEW HOPE
PUBLISHERS
Gospel-Centered. Missions-Driven.

BIRMINGHAM, ALABAMA

New Hope® Publishers
PO Box 12065
Birmingham, AL 35202-2065
NewHopeDigital.com
New Hope Publishers is a division of WMU®.

© 2014 by Taylor Field
All rights reserved. First printing 2014.
Printed in the United States of America.

No part of this publication may be reproduced, stored in a retrieval system, or
transmitted in any form or by any means—electronic, mechanical, photocopying,
recording, or otherwise—without the prior written permission of the publisher.

Library of Congress Product Control Number: 2013955341

Unless otherwise indicated, all Scripture quotations are from The Holy Bible,
English Standard Version, copyright © 2001 by Crossway Bibles, a division of
Good News Publishers. Used by permission. All rights reserved.
    Scripture quotations marked KJV are taken from The Holy Bible, King James
Version.
    Scripture quotations marked NKJV are taken from the New King James
Version. Copyright © 1982 by Thomas Nelson, Inc. Used by permission. All rights
reserved.
    Scripture quotations indicated by NIV are taken from the HOLY BIBLE, NEW
INTERNATIONAL VERSION®. NIV®. Copyright ©1973, 1978, 1984, 2011 by
Biblica, Inc.® Used by permission. All rights reserved worldwide.

Cover Design: Michel Lê
Interior Design: Glynese Northam

ISBN-10: 1-59669-405-X
ISBN-13: 978-1-59669-405-7
N144111 • 0414 • 3M1

Dedicated to

the hundreds of servers at the Graffiti sites,
who have taught me so much.

"Unless we act out what we believe,
we don't even believe it."

—attributed to THOMAS MERTON

# Contents

Acknowledgments

— To Susan, my wife, and to my sons and daughters-in-law, Freeman, Candace, Owen, and Krista, who all remind me that right side up may be upside down.

— To the workers at New Hope Publishers, especially Andrea Mullins and Joyce Dinkins, for being willing to look at familiar things and find the unfamiliar.

— To my co-workers at Graffiti, who turn devotion inside out and upside down every day.

introduction
Time for a Reset

"He has sent me to bind up the brokenhearted, to proclaim liberty to the captives, and the opening of the prison to those who are bound" (ISAIAH 61:1).

"If you board the wrong train, it is no use running along the corridor in the other direction."

—DIETRICH BONHOEFFER

Starting with the Hate Stuff

God hates our signs of devotion. He despises them. He finds our worship disgusting. The whole thing makes Him tired. It is boring to Him. I didn't say these things. God did.

Unless we do certain things, our devoted worship is, well, simply beyond His endurance. I know these statements sound harsh, but they are in the Bible a number of times. Just stay with me on this for a while.

Abraham Joshua Heschel was a rabbi who lost three sisters and his mother in World War II due to the Nazi regime. During and after the war, he continued to brood deeply about the Hebrew Scriptures. In writing about the prophets, he made a comment that struck home for me. He said that the Bible often seems out of proportion. Some things seem very important to God that don't seem so important to us. Clearly, thousands of years ago, some people were oppressed by those who had more. This fact seems to us, as we read about it, only to be a typical social dynamic. It seems to be more of a misdemeanor. To God, Heschel says, it is a catastrophe.

A serious, horrible catastrophe, a threat to the world. It is still happening today. Many things just don't seem like such a big deal to us as we read the Bible. The topic of sexual ethics in the Bible seems to be blown way out of proportion—to us, in our culture, the sins sometimes seem minor. Worshipping a graven image in the Bible is another area of emphasis that looks way overdone to some of us. But these things, as serious as they may be, are not the things that make God sick. There is something else that really turns Him off, that really disgusts him. In fact, He finds this other thing quite revolting and talks about it more than once. As I said, it has to do with worship.

Let me put together a couple of working definitions as we walk through these next few pages. *Devotion* is a loyalty or enthusiasm for a person or a cause. More specifically, *devotion* can be an act of religious observance or prayer. *Worship* is a related term. It can be seen as the array of ceremonies and prayers by which reverence to a deity is expressed. In this book, I will use the two words interchangeably.

In the Bible, examples of *worship* and *devotion* are things such as *offerings, incense, observance of new moons and Sabbaths, spreading out the hands in prayer, feasts, solemn assemblies, songs,* and *the study of the Scripture.* If we were to adapt these terms to our own time, we might say examples of worship and devotion are things such as *church services, study groups, conferences, Christian concerts, quiet times, conventions, praise songs,* and so forth. Surely these acts honor God, and speak the language of the heart. Not quite.

There is something else we must do, or these activities of worship are repugnant to God. In this matter, God gets quite personal and specific. In the first chapter of Isaiah, we see one example of the problem. When the people make offerings in their worship to God, God says He has had enough. He asks that they bring no more offerings, because the offerings are empty. Imagine a pastor today telling the people to bring no more offerings. God says that He finds incense, the sign at that time of their worship, to be an abomination. Remember that incense was the very thing the people brought to honor God. By calling it an abomination, He said it disgusted Him.

Yet God's words get even stronger. In fact, God says He cannot even endure the sin in their serious gatherings and special times together. We know that God is love, and so the next words are hard to handle. God hates — *hates* — the selected times of gathering for worship. These times have become a burden to Him. God says He is tired, weary of carrying them. In a sense, He calls our worship times a bore. In the context of the Bible, doesn't God enjoy our gatherings for Him? On the contrary, God says that no matter how many times we pray, He will not listen.

Strong words spoken directly from God to His people — almost like shock therapy. Let's read these four verses word for word:

> *When you come to appear before me,*
> *who has required of you*
> *this trampling of the courts?*
> *Bring no more vain offerings;*
> *incense is an abomination to me.*
> *New moon and Sabbath and the calling of convocations —*
> *I cannot endure iniquity and solemn assembly.*
> *Your new moons and your appointed feasts*
> *my soul hates;*
> *they have become a burden to me;*
> *I am weary of bearing them.*
> *When you spread out your hands,*
> *I will hide my eyes from you;*
> *even though you make many prayers,*
> *I will not listen:*
> *Your hands are full of blood.*
>
> —Isaiah 1:12–15

Sounds pretty harsh, doesn't it? But God doesn't end there. He gives gentle, loving correction. When we do what He says, we bring a balance back to worship and devotion. Sometimes, when we are taking our worship to the next level, when the music and the preaching take us to a new phase in our adoration of God, this corrective may seem mundane and routine. Yet without this corrective, all our worship becomes a calamity, an abnormality. Maybe the corrective seemed out of proportion to the people at that time too.

Finally, we get the corrective. In the very next lines of Isaiah, God tells the people to wash themselves clean. Unless we do the following things, all our religious activities, no matter how fervent and intense, are insulting to God:

> Cease to do evil,
>   learn to do good;
> seek justice,
>   correct oppression;
> bring justice to the fatherless,
>   plead the widow's cause.
>
> —ISAIAH 1:16–17

That's it. That is the instruction. Somehow, these fatherless people and these widows are extremely, extremely important to God. It is almost as if nothing else matters if these people are ignored. All the other bells and whistles of worship—the sound systems, the overhead projector, the preaching, the wonderful singing—all mean nothing if these people are overlooked. Really, the worship is worse than nothing. It becomes repugnant to God. These fatherless and widows were the people who were most vulnerable, who were least protected in the society Isaiah is speaking to. These were the people living in the shadows, those not in the center of society's attention. God tells us clearly that we are to seek justice, fairness, so that there is a level playing field for all people. Even if none of these instructions makes sense, God says we can "learn to do good." I am so glad that if we are not doing good, then it is something we can learn.

It's Just New to You

*I*n a sense, God turns our normal expressions of devotion and worship upside down and inside out. We think of worship as singing songs, hearing the Word, taking notes. However, unless we take a stand for those who in trouble, we have missed the boat. By taking a stand, I mean doing tangible things for and with those in need. In this book, I will call specific acts of love for others *service*. In the world of the Bible, this service is the tangible expression of God's love. Service is upside-down devotion. Somehow, we need to put the real concept of service back into the phrase we use so often—the *worship service*. This service points us back to action. From our context, this action may sometimes feel like extreme action. But when we listen again to our most astonishing and remarkable God, that extreme action puts us into a new balance.

The root word of *devotion* can mean "related to a vow" (*de* + *votus*). We are "the devoted" in our loyalty to God in the context of a vow. But somehow this word *devoted* has deteriorated to an expression of the trappings of the vow. We need a new word. To regain the sense of action for those who are "de-voted," I am calling those who are in balance the ones who are learning to *do* good. They are the "*do*-voted." There is simply something we have to do. If we refuse to do the things God tells us to do, we become the "dead-voted." Remember Ananias and Sapphira who came to worship as hypocrites in the New Testament, claiming to have given something they had not? It caused their deaths (Acts 5:1–11).

We want to get our lives in sync again. We want not just to have the *form* of religion, we want the *power* again. Deep in our hearts we want to have integrity. We want to turn devotion upside down, and become the "do-voted" rather than merely the "de-voted."

A friend of mine who grew up in the Bronx has helped me greatly. He has worked with several large Christian organizations. He has noticed that there are waves of new leadership and waves of new ideas in the organizations every few years. A new vocabulary and a new emphasis emerges that for a while is promoted as the very thing that will resolve the issues or achieve the goal. He has often discovered that the thing promoted is something that was already done under a different vocabulary years before. He is patient. "This is not new," he will say, "it is just new to you."

Turning worship upside down isn't new. It was done by the prophets thousands of years ago at different times. I suppose that in every generation there is the need to think deeply about what worship is. The natural enthusiasm of one generation becomes the tedious liturgy of the next. When worship becomes a formula, when the words come easy, when the expectations fall into little categories, it is time to think again.

As my friend said, of course none of this is new. We see different groups dealing with the challenge of worship at different points in the Scripture. For example, in Isaiah 58, God continues working to retool our understanding. In the context of our commonly accepted understanding of worship, the words hardly even make sense. This chapter portrays the people of God as *delighting* to draw near to Him, especially in their eagerness to fast and move toward God in prayer. "Yet they seek me daily and delight to know my ways" (Isaiah 58:2). The people feel that bowing down and fasting is a sign that they have humbled themselves. Isn't this what God wants?

Again, God challenges what the people think is so devotional. We focus on the outward circumstances, but God deals with motives. He says that the people use their times of fasting for their own pleasure, and to oppress workers, and to quarrel and strike out. He seems to want to revamp their times of fasting completely and say that the real fast and real worship is to undo the straps of burden, to let the oppressed go free, to break every chain that brings someone down. "'Is this not the fast I choose: . . . to let the oppressed go free, and to break every yoke?'" (Isaiah 58:6). Oddly enough, God implies that true fasting is to be involved with feeding the poor and providing housing for them and clothing, and not to ignore the needs of our own family. God asks if a real fast isn't "to share your bread with the hungry and bring the homeless into your house; when you see the naked to cover him?" (Isaiah 58:7). Notice how specific God is in describing the acts of service He is looking for in true fasting. It is as though God is working to remodel our hearts' perceptions of Him. The words probably sounded strange to the people that Isaiah was speaking to. It still seems a bit strange to us today. Worship just isn't quite what we thought worship was.

Isaiah 58 is such a wonderful chapter. Once we do the things God tells us to do, the feeding and housing and clothing stuff, we become the "do-voted" again. Our lives and worship are restored to freshness and productivity. We are "like a watered garden, like a spring of water." Once we are in balance, we will bless the city, and even be called "the restorer of streets to dwell in" (Isaiah 58:11, 12). Equilibrium is restored to our lives and to our city.

The entire Book of Amos gives the same challenge to us and turns devotion on its head repeatedly. It describes an area bustling with all kinds of religious activity, and yet these activities are basically irrelevant. Shockingly, once again God speaks in the language of disgust and hate:

> *I hate, I despise your feasts,*
> > *and I take no delight in your solemn assemblies.*
> *Even though you offer me your burnt offerings and grain offerings,*
> > *I will not accept them;*
> *and the peace offerings of your fattened animals,*
> > *I will not look upon them.*
> *Take away from me the noise of your songs;*
> > *to the melody of your harps I will not listen.*
>
> —AMOS 5:21–23

Sound familiar? Gatherings, potluck fellowships, offerings, music—they are all included in what He finds despicable. In the same vein as before, God gives a loving corrective. He turns devotion on its head:

> *But let justice roll down like waters,*
> > *And righteousness like an ever-flowing stream.*
>
> —AMOS 5:24

The Book of Micah asks the same sort of question. Micah asks how he is to come before the Lord, how he is to bow down in worship. He goes to extremes to describe what he could do to lay himself before the Lord, to offer thousands of animals and ten thousands of rivers of oil, and even the unthinkable of offering his firstborn child. In his general culture, these were all expected ways to worship God; surrounding pagan cultures did sacrifice their children; and Micah exaggerates the limits in his display of devotion. Again, God works to give Micah and the people a kind of retooling of devotion. He gives Micah a simple answer:

> He has told you, O man, what is good;
>> And what does the Lord require of you
> but to do justice, to love kindness,
>> and to walk humbly with your God?
>
> —MICAH 6:8

Once more, the first thing is to *do* justice, to *do* something for justice and fairness. Once again, it is to become the do-voted, not just the de-voted. We can cite a whole list of other Bible examples before us, but I think we get the point.

But I Can't Even Clean My Own Bathroom

*T*he spirit of the New Testament is the same. Jesus makes very clear that just fervently shouting out, "Lord, Lord," is not entering the kingdom of heaven. That person shouting, "Lord, Lord," may be doing all the things of the time that makes one think of devotion. At that moment in time those special things were prophesying, casting out demons, and performing the miraculous. But if the person didn't *do* the will of the Father, that person had missed the boat (Matthew 7:21–23). Astonishing.

Jesus tells a great story of devotion turned inside out when He talks about the good Samaritan. Here is this brutally mugged man on the side of the road, and the priest and the temple helper just walk right by. I think of them weighed down with all their responsibilities for helping with worship, for assisting people to adore God in the temple. Perhaps they justified their actions to themselves, thinking of all the worshippers that were waiting on them and depended on them in the city. They needed to move along in order to help those people waiting to glorify God. Yet they missed the point and failed the test, finding their own tasks more important than helping a person in need right in front of them (Luke 10:25–37).

James, the brother of Jesus, won't let it go either. He portrays the person who uses the language of devotion and has all the right words, but does nothing else.

If a brother or sister is poorly clothed and lacking in daily food, and one of you says to them, 'Go in peace, be warmed and filled,' without giving them the things needed for the body, what good is that?"

(JAMES 2:15–16).

Once we start seeing God's challenge to us to have true worship, we begin to see it in the whole Bible, from Genesis to Revelation. It jumps out at us everywhere. We fervently pray for revival in our nation, and Proverbs 21:13 springs out at us: "Whoever closes his ear to the cry of the poor will himself cry out and not be answered." We get into intense study and arguments about issues related to the Word of God, and find that Jesus says the Pharisees applied the Scriptures to the tiniest matters, but "neglected the weightier matters of the law: justice and mercy and faithfulness" (Matthew 23:23). There's that word *justice* again. The references go on and on.

If you have read this far, you may be having some of the same feelings I had. "I can't even find time to clean my own bathroom, much less do all this kind of stuff, like fighting injustice and helping the oppressed. Isn't this instruction just a new form of legalism? I feel worn out enough as it is." True. This could all be just another form of telling us all the things we *should* do.

I think sometimes about what the preacher said at the first sermon in our new mission building in New York City. "There is nothing I can do that is good enough to get me into heaven, and there is nothing I can do that is bad enough to keep me out of heaven." That is the place to start. God provides and we receive. Nothing that comes from heaven is earned. Everything is achieved by trust. Yet as we trust, God gives us tender instructions when things have gotten out of whack. Part of our journey with God is being honest and saying that something has gone wrong.

When We Feel Lost Midway . . .

*S*o much is different for us than for those in the Bible. We don't offer animals. We may not fast much, or use a lot of oil in our worship anymore. We don't observe the new moon, or disfigure our faces to look religious like the Pharisees. Still, as we read the Bible, we sometimes sense that we need something, that something is not quite right in our own experience.

I love the fact that when our electronic devices go awry, there is something anyone can do to begin fixing the problem. It is simply called *a reset*. We can restart the computer, or take the battery out of the device, or press some tiny button. Essentially, a reset clears the system of any pending errors. I don't understand it. Sometimes I think in life that the first thing we need to do is not to do anything. We just need to stop, and turn to God and ask for a reset. A reset somehow recalibrates us and gets us back to our normal operating process, when things have gradually gone amiss; we don't know how or why.

This sense of getting off course is not something that is special to our current electronic passions. It's always been there. We see it in the greatest literature. In the opening of Dante's *Divine Comedy* (part 1, *The Inferno*), for example, the author explains that midway through his life, he finds himself somehow in a dark wood, where the right road was wholly gone. Most of us have had that experience in life at some time, having started out strong, but somehow in the middle of things, feeling that we are not quite on track. So maybe the first thing we need to do is to just stop and admit that midway we have gotten a bit lost in the woods. The trees have been so big and compelling and the paths seem so various that we don't quite see the forest anymore. We don't even remember what the forest really looks like.

Perhaps this is what God is seeking to tell us, that somehow we have gone astray in worship, and that it has happened so gradually, so steadily, that we have not even noticed it. We, as a group of His believers, have developed what we feel is an astute sense of right and wrong, and cultivate the ability to discern the boundaries of what we are to do. With all our training and resources, we may have become quite articulate in describing these boundaries. However, my wife has put it very succinctly when she said, "It is not as important to *judge* people rightly as to *treat* people rightly."

We find that if we only focus on the techniques of worship and the language of faith, all we have is an amputated limb, something separated from the body of Christ. It is not enough. If we keep reading the Bible, the Bible will prod us. The Bible sometimes says it is time to turn worship inside out, to come at it again. I think we find that when we turn worship inside out, we find service on the inside. We know that if we only do service, only focus on tangible acts, we end up just giving away our emptiness. We will follow a "social gospel" that becomes all social with no gospel. Yet on the other hand, without service, worship becomes something hollow too.

It Is All About Context

*W*e find that those who value service a lot sometimes have a hard time even discussing the issues with those who are involved greatly with the worship aspect of our lives. The "service people" cannot understand a cost of a new sound system and its value in worship, when they see that the same money could have gone to help those most in need. By the same token, people involved in the acts of worship may see those involved in service as prickly or condemning, people who have forgotten the generosity of simply pouring out expensive perfume for our Lord. Focusing on doing can make it sound as though we are descending into a contrast between law and grace. The doers seem like legalists. It all depends on context.

But context means a lot in situations like that. As a young man, my wife and I moved to work in a ministry in an area that seemed to thrive in a certain kind of lawlessness. People lived in abandoned buildings. I remember looking out the window of the apartment we took over for ministry, and watching men take advantage of prostitutes, poor woman desperate for the next fix.

The lack of accountability seemed horrible to me. Men made no commitment to women, but wandered from apartment to apartment as women bore the burden of raising children, sons and daughters of yet another generation of individuals who barely knew their fathers. Lying and stealing were common. I remember simply allowing a person in need to make a phone call at our ministry during the first weeks I was there. Only later did I realize that in addition to making the call, he had put our only answering machine in his sleeping bag and walked out. "Everything has wings," was one saying on the street. Robberies of unguarded tools, money, purses, cameras, and other portable items were frequent.

At the same time, the very people who robbed us might use all the evangelical language I was used to. They would use the slogan of the time, "born again," and talk about being "saved," while dealing drugs and beating up their girlfriends.

I came to realize in a kind of primal way that stealing wasn't cool, it was ugly. Lying wasn't chic, it was boring. Prostitutes weren't glamorous like in the slick movies, they were gaunt and pathetic. Immorality wasn't liberating, it was boorish, and ultimately devastating to the children. In a world that seemed so chaotic, I learned to love the Ten Commandments, the necessary structure for society to exist long term. Those commandments didn't seem legalistic to me at all. They seemed wonderful. I tended to see the TV with new eyes—the endless glorification of cops and bandits who broke the rules didn't seem so cool anymore. I became suspicious of the pervasive mocking of morality because of my own context. The repetitive challenges to traditional rules so common on TV started looking to me like lazy thinking, a short-term offer that refused to think through the consequences. Because of my day-to-day experience in a place where many of those "conventional rules" were lacking, I saw how important such rules were in society. I came to love the basic laws that we were to obey.

I remember a woman who was in a coma for a long time due to the toll constant drug use had taken on her body. In the coma, she dreamed that she had died. She dreamed that she was in hell. But hell was just her same neighborhood, the worst of her neighborhood without requirements, where gangs roamed without any protection from outside, where wild dogs went from street to street with no owners, where ugliness and selfishness reigned on every corner with no restraining laws. She saw it as a horrible place. Because I was living in a neighborhood where many of those accepted laws were gone, what she said made sense to me. Her vision of hell was that place I had seen, without structure, without law, without accountability.

My younger sister helped me finally to understand the power of context in spiritual matters. She was, in contrast to my lawless environment, sometimes in a context where everyone seemed to be a Christian. The rules were honored, but then the transgression of even the smallest cultural rule seemed to bring extreme guilt and condemnation. Of course, in this world, some of the Christians who seemed to uphold the rules and the laws the most—they turned out to be a disappointment too.

Sometimes, in my sister's experience, these laws seemed to be a confining, even oppressive, legalism. God's grace liberated her from this kind of world that earlier only led to further self-recrimination. Therefore, she might wince if I talked about the need of the commandments of God. In a sense, my sister had heard all of that before, and it wasn't that good. However, I saw the consequences when the laws were all gone. In my context, grace was used as an excuse. In her context, the laws were used as hypocrisy. My sister and I could barely understand each other because our experiences were so different.

Three Tough Theologians

*W*hat happened between me and my sister can happen when people in the church talk about worship and service. Our context determines our opinions. We need to be gentle with each other. It is hard for us to stay balanced. We tend to veer from one side to another. Martin Luther once said that "the world is like a drunken peasant; if someone helps him into the saddle on one side, he will fall off on the other side."

So when we talk about service, some people can only hear that we are falling into a ditch of legalism, judging everything by what humans do. Sometimes we do become legalistic. For me, Martin Luther is once again very helpful here. No one could talk about grace like Martin Luther. He would go to extremes. To make the point about grace, he once wrote his good friend that no sin could separate us from Him, even if we, among other things, committed 1,000 murders in one day.

When Luther was forced to hide in the castle at Wartburg, the power of his words on grace seemed to be unleashed in his own town of Wittenberg. When Luther returned, he felt that things had gotten out of hand. He preached a sermon series about law in response. He said a faith without love is not faith at all. Then he preached a series on the Ten Commandments, which seemed the opposite of his grace message. But once again, everything depends on context.

From one perspective, Luther's powerful teaching on grace and law from the Bible eventually degenerated sometimes through the centuries into a weak Lutheranism. I fear that many of our own churches move in the same direction. In the twentieth century, Dietrich Bonhoeffer, an heir of the great biblical truths from Luther and the Reformation and a Lutheran pastor himself, saw the dangers and described the platitudes of a lightly evangelical church as a kind of "cheap grace." This was a grace composed of words that cost nothing and eventually meant nothing.

Albert Schweitzer, the missionary doctor to Africa in the twentieth century, also brooded over the meaning of the message of the Reformation and the Bible. Although many of his views vary from an evangelical view, he saw the dangers of a faith only founded on what Luther saw as primary—the Apostle Paul's idea of justification by faith. As he read and reread Paul's letters, he saw the dying and rising with Christ as the real defining message. Schweitzer was struck by the passages of Paul's writings which indicated that one could fall away and fail in the process, backsliding or drifting from Christ. Like others before him, he was concerned that without that possibility of failing, then ethics fails, because if everything is forgiven no matter what, then nothing is required. And for Schweitzer, ethics was at the heart of worship. He might say to those who depended on an easy grace, "Go back and look at the first chapter of Isaiah again."

People who focus on worship sometimes rightly think that people who focus on service are legalistic, but of course, it is all knit together. The Reformation image of fire and heat is a helpful metaphor for describing this balance. Faith is the fire and works are the heat. If I go to a cabin in the mountains and it is very cold, I don't look around for heat. I look around for the materials to start a fire. If I start a fire, the heat will come.

When we have the faith, the works will come. But if there is a fire and no heat, something is wrong.

Sometimes we just need to blow on the embers of the fire when we see how cold and lifeless the room has become. This is simply another way to say we need a reset.

What I Wish I Knew Earlier

Don Miller tells a story that I cannot get out of my head. It's in his book on growing up without a father. He was on a flight to Portland and he was using his headphones and found a channel that connected him to the conversation the pilots were having with other planes. He was surprised to find out what the pilot and copilot were talking about most of the time. They were either talking to the pilot who was an hour ahead of them, or they were talking to the pilot who was an hour behind them. The pilots want to find out what kind of turbulence and weather there was ahead, and they were telling the pilots behind them what kind of turbulence and weather to expect as they approached the next phase of their flight. Don Miller realized this is what life is like, listening to those ahead of you and speaking to those who are coming after you.

I have been focusing on finding tangible ways to express Christ's love for more than 35 years in urban areas—in Harlem, in Hong Kong, in San Francisco, and in the Lower East Side. Perhaps there is something I can say that will be helpful to the pilots behind me. The ten upside-down principles I share are the things I wish I had known when I started. Maybe that information can help those who are flying on the next current that is coming.

Of course, we don't want to learn everything by experience. I don't want to learn what a plane crash feels like. I don't want to know what boiling water feels like poured on my face. I don't want to know what it feels like to jump off a ten-story building. We couldn't survive a day if we had to learn everything by experience.

I remember hearing a quote attributed to Abraham Lincoln once that said a beautiful thing about writing and reading. Through it, he said, I can listen to those who came before me and talk to those who come after me. What an opportunity! I am so glad I have had the chance to listen to those who came before me. Now is my opportunity to talk to those who come after me as they think about real community work.

In other words, what do I know now concerning service that I wish I knew when I started? If I could meet myself 35 years ago, what could I say to myself that might be helpful? The things in this book are some of the things I would say to myself. (You can see appendix B if you want to read a cheat sheet—what I would tell you if I only had five minutes to tell you my personal rules for community ministry.) This is not a book for those who simply want to serve a Thanksgiving meal for the homeless once a year and then go about their normal business. These are lessons learned alongside those who have gotten deeply involved in the messiness of the ones who have the least in our communities. The principles are for people who are in it for the long haul.

Breaking Out with Jimmy

*I*t is so easy to get into the routines of what we know of worship, and forget the freshness of its freedom. Last year I thought I knew what worship was. Every week I submitted my little outline of my sermon to the worship team. Every week we worked on components of the worship. We had the audiovisual team, the music team, the setup people, the greeters, the worship service leaders, the printer of the bulletin, and on and on. I started feeling like I was pretty busy and that my time was so important. It's funny how we talk ourselves into these feelings, over and over, no matter what our situation is.

For more than 20 years, we had gone to a nursing home close to our mission to lead a service there. Sometimes there were very few people at the service. Sometimes we just kind of rushed in and did something quickly and rushed out. We had other things to do. Sometimes we took the time to go talk to some of the people in their rooms.

Jimmy never did come to the worship services. Not once. He never turned the pages of the songbook. He never listened to the Scripture in our worship time, or heard the preaching. Yet I still went by to see him because I remembered him from years earlier. He used to hang out in the park and he used to come to one of the free meals the mission provided. He was a free spirit. I remembered Jimmy particularly because he used to walk around with a baby squirrel in his pocket. No kidding.

It had fallen out of a tree and he had become its mother. The squirrel would sit in his shirt pocket as he ate his meal at our mission.

By the time I visited Jimmy in his little room, he was pretty depressed. He was not really old enough to be in a nursing home, from my point of view. One of his legs was gone. Who knows what can really happen in life. From Jimmy's perspective, he says the doctors never told him they were going to amputate his leg when he went in for what he thought was relatively minor surgery. Jimmy, who loved his freedom, woke up without a leg, confined to a dingy cell in a large institution. He was a lame, middle-aged man stuck in a nursing home with nothing to do and not much to hope for. No wonder he was depressed. He tried to tell the doctor about it, so they gave him some medication for depression.

He said he just wanted to get out of that nursing home. He wouldn't say much to me, but sometimes he would say something like this: "All I want is to go out to the park one more time and sit there and have a cup of coffee." I nodded and made a mental note to try to do that for him sometime, when I had time. It's hard to describe how the organizations in New York can make a church worker feel hopeless. I just knew in my heart that to get permission for Jimmy to go out, even once, would require a bunch of requests, letters, certifications, delays, and waivers at a variety of offices. I had seen it before. So I procrastinated. I was going to work on it one day.

Eventually the nursing home was scheduled to close. Morale was down and many of the patients didn't quite know where they were going to be assigned. I went for my last visit there, and spent some time with some of the people who were more talkative and pleasant. Then I thought of Jimmy. The visits to Jimmy were a little dreary. Sometimes he would just sit there with nothing to say. *Did I have time to visit him one more time? Maybe I could squeeze in a half hour.*

I thought of all the papers I had to sign back at the office, the emails, the meetings, the recommendations, the finances, the worship preparation I had to do. I didn't really have time—the things I needed to do seemed so important to me. Then I thought of Jimmy and his best days with his squirrel, and I decided I would visit him once more. I couldn't just think about it. I had to do something, even if it was just for a half hour. It was one of the best decisions I ever made in ministry. I decided to ask, on the spur of the moment, if I could take Jimmy out. It seemed like a futile effort, but I steeled myself to try. I asked the nurse at the desk about the process for getting approval for a nonfamily member to take someone out. She didn't even look up. She gave me a form, and said I had to talk to the main nurse on the floor. At just that time, the main nurse walked down the hall. I stopped her and gave her the form. It was like the parting of the Red Sea waters. She smiled, signed the form, and directed me to another office to get approval. The person just happened to be there and signed the form with no questions. I couldn't believe it was going so quickly.

Before I knew it I was racing down the hall to Jimmy's room. I thought of Jesus, sharing the heart of His ministry by reading from Isaiah—it was all about telling good news to the poor and proclaiming liberty to the captives. I got to share some good news that day. I burst into Jimmy's room. As always, he was lying on the bed in a stupor watching game shows. I said, "Get in your wheelchair, Jimmy, we are breaking out of here!" I have never seen anyone jump up with so much agility. He got himself in the wheelchair, and we sailed out of there. I flashed the form I had gotten signed at each checkpoint, and locked doors began to open for us. No one stopped us. We felt like Peter and the angel walking out as the prison doors opened. We got out the final door, and as if on cue, the chain-link fence gate swung open for us, so that we made it to the street.

Jimmy roared with laughter. So did I. I hadn't heard him laugh since he was in the nursing home. He began to sing as we cruised down the sidewalk. We were free. We went to the corner store and got two cups of hot, steaming coffee. We went to the park, where he had spent so much of his life. He told me again that in all his years at the nursing home, he had never once been permitted out of the building. This was his first time. We sat on his old park bench, and listened to the birds, and drank our coffee and chatted. Freedom and the coffee were a heady mix for him. He wouldn't stop talking he was so happy. We both were. He talked about God and his buddies on the street and his squirrel and his memories. Somehow, I felt as though this time in the park was the real reason I had wanted to become a minister of Christ so many years ago. As I sat in the park, I was so glad I hadn't gone back to the office to prepare my sermon points that were already late. So what? Jimmy and I sat in the park holding our coffee like Communion. In our own upside-down way, we worshipped together.

principle #1
We Are Light, Not Lightning

"And his servants came near and spoke to him, and said, 'My father, if the prophet had told you to do something great, would you not have done it?'" (2 KINGS 5:13 NKJV).

"All that is gold does not glitter; not all those that wander are lost."

—J. R. R. TOLKIEN, *THE FELLOWSHIP OF THE RING*

A Fistfight During Worship

*L*ast Sunday we had a brawl in our worship service. Just as I was getting ready to step up to preach, I was summoned to the other side of the church with a breathy urgency. By the time I got over there, a woman was pressing her hand into the face of an angry man and loudly rebuking him in the name of Jesus. The man was shouting and cursing. I think the woman was using some pretty colorful words in between her prayers too. The wide-eyed children in our worship service were picking up quite a church vocabulary! The woman's boyfriend had been shuffled away because he had already caused a ruckus. The worship leader sang louder and louder, though the congregation was glued to the bustling bodies in the back.

I wondered what the first-time visitors were thinking. Not exactly the guest-friendly service I was hoping for. The shouting woman was still not responding to my request to stop, nor to anyone else. Slowly the group of fighting, tussling people was moving to the exit, as the music played on. The stream of people gurgled down the stairs and spilled out into the street; then the fighters slowly began to separate. As I squared off with one of the most vocal participants on the sidewalk, I suddenly remembered that I was supposed to be preaching inside.

I turned around to rush back into the church, but as I did, I saw a solitary, lonely figure hobbling away from the fray and the church service. I stopped for an instant, and then I turned again and sprinted through the door. I eventually slowed my run to a walk, and gravely strolled up to preach. The worship leader was still bravely leading songs, though the congregation's heart was somewhere else. After the service, everyone was talking about who did what, who started it, and who dropped the f-bomb the most.

But those were not the things I thought about the most. I kept thinking about that solitary figure walking down the street, quietly cursing. His name was James. He, apparently, was the one who had started the fight. Yet most people didn't know much more about him.

I knew a little bit more. He had some kind of short-term memory loss. He struggled to remember things that were just said. He had a lot of tricks to keep functioning in a social situation. One of his ways was humor. He would ask me his name, over and over, and laugh, pretending that I had forgotten his name. He was homeless, and talked to me about getting baptized. He had been coming regularly every Sunday, sitting alone. I don't know how he remembered when to come. When we talked, he was so excited because he had gotten a little work and had a place to stay for four nights.

Once, as we were speaking in private, he removed his knit cap to show me his head. His skull looked as though it had been horribly crushed. He said he was beaten up in Chicago and was in a coma for two months. He taught himself to read again using a Christian book. He didn't want pity. I admired him, with his sense of humor and his courage. That very morning, before the fight, he had asked for help with an eye infection. Someone had stuck their finger in his eye. Things weren't right and he was in a bad way. We were going to talk after the worship time.

For one brief moment on that sidewalk before I rushed back in, I stopped thinking about myself. I stopped being irritated at the disruption of our worship service. I wondered what that solitary figure, hobbling down the street, must have felt like. He didn't have any family to go to. He would probably just drift to another place. I wondered what his world felt like, as he faced another little failure. Then after that brief pause, I immediately thought about myself again, and what I would say and do as I rushed back in to deliver my "important" sermon in worship.

We all talked about "the fight" in the following days. That was the big drama for the week. The loudest actors in the fight got all the attention. But I imagine most of the time we fail to see the significant things, when there is theatrical emotion and tension. I couldn't forget the image of that sad man limping down the street, and I asked myself what had been most important to God that day in our worship. What was the rest of the day like for James, alone with his infected eye? The fight got all the press. In the end, James was ignored. Even though James had been attending church every week, he didn't come back the next Sunday. I haven't seen him since. There was no joyous baptism for James.

The Power of One Little Pronoun

As I said in the introduction, there were times in the Bible when God said he found His people's worship hateful, disgusting, because we had ignored the things that are so important to Him. Somehow now it seems as though it's time for a "reset." Something is not quite right. In the language of computers and smartphones, it is time to clear our system of pending errors and return to our "normal" condition. Where should we look in order to get back to what we were made to be?

Earlier this year, I was at another meeting in a string of back-to-back meetings on the third day of seemingly interminable meetings. I sat on the third row, slouched down, looking for a way to check my emails. My mood began to change, however, when a young Indian pastor from Queens began to speak about his church. One thing he said at the beginning made me forget all about emails.

He said, "Our church wants to be light, not lightning. Lightning brings a big flash, and then big thunder, and then it is gone. It gets a lot of attention, and then it is over. Sometimes it even does damage. But a light, like a city light, is not noticed, but quietly blesses the city, on and on."

That was it. The young pastor had formulated in a moment what I had been trying unsuccessfully to say for years. In service, we so often look for the lightning, the dramatic boom, something big. That's what takes our attention. That is what we can tell a story about. Unfortunately, after the flash, often there is little that remains. In the coming times, I see a group of young people yearning for real light, not just the short-term, loud, dramatic firebolt.

That same week, I had been talking to a man I will call José. He had spent 30 years in and out of prison and knew a lot about the street. If someone said anything about God, he would say in anger, "I *am* God." He started coming to some high school equivalency classes in our mission. He started talking to Kareem, our associate pastor. Kareem said, "Why don't you come to church? We would love to have you."

You never know what quiet little thing you say or do may touch someone. Kareem didn't say anything dramatic, or necessarily profound. There was no thunder. When he went home that night, he probably didn't think anything important had happened that day.

But it had. For José, somehow, the fact that Kareem had said, "*We* would love to have you" instead of "*I* would love to have you" had a deep impact on him. He had quietly watched Kareem through the days before. He watched Kareem's kindness in the routine things. Something about Kareem had touched his heart. That little pronoun, *we*, quiet and undramatic as it was, became the beginning of a deep experience with Christ for José.

After accepting Christ, José sat with Kareem and said a prayer for Kareem. He said, "This is the first real prayer I have ever prayed for someone else in my life. Every prayer before this one was when I was shooting up. I would stick the needle in my arm and pray, 'Lord, make this shot kill me.'"

Quiet, little, routine, mundane ways in service can have a different effect on people than big events we plan in order to change lives. We can't truly monitor them. We often don't even know they happen. Kareem was blessed that José told him about the changes in his life. Often, we never know.

How to Take the Place of a Drama King

God has a lot of different ways to speak, and uses a lot of different personalities. I would call Elijah in the Bible a "drama king" (1 Kings 17 to 2 Kings 2). I don't mean this in a bad way. He just had a flair for historic staging. With his weird hair, outfit, and leather belt out in the desert, he certainly drew attention. When he appeared and said there was no more rain, there was no more rain. He faced off against the king and then, dramatically dousing his sacrifice with water, he called fire down on his sacrifice. He ran distances similar to a marathon. When soldiers came, he called fire down on them too. He even went out with a bang, going up in a whirlwind with chariots of fire. This was Elijah's way — sometimes big bangs are all people can experience. In the midst of battle, bombs may be the only thing one can hear.

Elisha was a little different. We only know that Elisha was with Elijah and "poured water on his hands" — in other words, served the prophet Elijah (1 Kings 19 to 2 Kings 13). At the end of Elijah's life, Elisha asked for a double portion of Elijah's spirit, and we are told he got it. But Elisha's manner was his own. It is always hard to take over the position of a charismatic leader. Elisha seemed to do the quieter things. He made some bad water wholesome. He made some poisonous soup edible. He multiplied bread for 100 people. He recovered a lost iron ax head. Even in battle, he worked it out so that the enemy surrendered, and then had his own people give them food.

The contrasts in the story of the commander Naaman are my favorite (2 Kings 5:1–19). Just as in our lives, often in the Bible one part of a person's life is going great, while the other part of the person's life is terrible. Naaman was a big shot. His career was exceptional, but at the same time he had leprosy. I like to imagine Naaman's entourage coming up to Elisha's prophet's hut. We are told Naaman has brought 150 pounds (not ounces) of gold and 750 pounds of silver. We might say that is a rather visible amount of spending money to carry with you.

I like to imagine Elisha's servant quietly coming out, stepping over all the equipment and maneuvering around the pack animals. The servant made no impressive welcoming speeches to Naaman and his parade. He softly told Naaman to wash seven times in the Jordan River. That's it.

Commander Naaman was understandably furious. He wanted something dramatic. He wanted Elisha to do something *for* him. He expected Elisha to come out and wave his hands over the problem, do some religious hocus pocus. What's more, compared to the rivers in his own country, the Jordan River was puny.

His officers finally reasoned with him that if Elisha had asked for something dramatic and sacrificial, Naaman would have surely done it. Yet Elisha's imperative was something quiet and simple.

I imagine his entourage all going with him to the Jordan River. Of course, Naaman has to take off all the rich clothing of a commander. He has to stand in the water, and all of his subordinates could see that he was what he was—a leper. Then he had to do the same, simple, mundane task over and over and over and over and over and over and over again. Seven times. Then his skin became as healthy as a child's.

Naaman went back to give Elisha a gift. Think of the magnificent ministry Elisha could have done with that money. Once again, Elisha declined. What he had done wasn't the kind of thing a person could pay for. Elisha seemed to be more into the quiet light, not the lightning.

In this line of thought, the prophet Isaiah is helpful too. God spoke to the people very clearly using an image of water. Don't go after the big, showy alliances that you think will save you. Before you know it, you will have too much drama, which will engulf you like a huge, mighty river. God offered them the "waters of Shiloah that flow gently," but the people refused them. Shiloah was the small channel of water they knew about, right there in the city area. Probably not flashy enough for them (Isaiah 8:5–8).

The people continue to rush around, trying to find some dramatic answer to all their problems by making the right alliances. God tells them that there is a lower-key way to handle the problems. "In returning and rest you shall be saved; in quietness and in trust shall be your strength" (30:15). God tells them again, that by trying to find the dramatic answer, their destruction will be dramatic (30:16–17).

A Boxer, a Bishop, and a Hobbit

*E*ven in the natural world, the quiet, steady things are often what bring the big changes in the end. When I was a student in Berlin during the 1970s, Marxist analysis was all the rage. I understood very little of it, but I remember students would state this axiom: "Quantitative change leads to qualitative change." Water gets colder and colder by degrees, and eventually it becomes ice. Darkness gets lighter and lighter, and eventually it becomes day. In ministry in the city, we are often working by degrees, slowly, step-by-step. One day, after a long time, we wake up, and the quality of things, their substance, has changed—we didn't even realize when.

From this perspective, long-term, low-key events have their own value. We usually look for quick results. Yet sometimes these results are deceiving. We may need to turn things upside down. Things that take a long time may need to grab our attention, not the sudden success. I tease some other Christian workers who, like myself, have been doing something for a long time and therefore are ignored by those looking for the next big explosion. I tell them that we are not old—we just have "longevity capital."

When we aim at simply being light, quietly plugging away for a long time, all the verses about endurance and patience in the Bible come alive again for us. "For you have need of endurance," the Book of Hebrews tells us, "so that when you have done the will of God you may receive what is promised" (10:36). Keep plugging away with the quantitative steps. The qualitative change will come.

Usually in the life of service, in turning worship upside down, it is more important to keep plodding along than to look for the quick win. We refuse to get discouraged by the temporary setback. My co-worker and I quote Proverbs 24:16 to each other: "For the righteous falls seven times and rises again, but the wicked stumble in times of calamity." We love to cite the boxer Floyd Patterson, knocked down seven times in one round of a championship fight. He eventually fought again and regained the championship title. He said, "They said I was the fighter who got knocked down the most, but I also got up the most." That quality of getting up, again and again, in victory or in defeat, will often bring the qualitative change we pray for. If we give up when lightning doesn't work, we've missed it.

At our mission, we sometimes talk about the "habit of doing well" in doing our work. Some writers know the truth of the quiet way. In Les Misérables by Victor Hugo, the kind bishop has a quiet habit of doing well. When he is robbed by the man just out of prison, he tells the authorities that the silver that was robbed was actually a gift to the robber. This act of kindness changes the robber's life, and the rest of the story is about the goodness of that convict. However, it seems that the bishop never knows about the dramatic change. That is the way life is. The bishop just had the habit of doing well, and kept doing it.

Humans aren't so great at evaluating success. We often think that lightning is the sign of great victory. In reality, it may be, and it may not be. Our culture loved the movies from the book The Lord of the Rings, but the writer J. R. R. Tolkien made it very clear that the great battles fought by Aragorn and Gandalf were really a sideshow. The real victory involves a grindingly tedious journey by two little hobbits, plugging away toward Mordor, unnoticed and unheralded.

The prophet Isaiah understood that combination of quiet action and refusing to get discouraged. He talked about that special Servant who was to come in a passage that we now understand as messianic foreshadowing. Isaiah describes the Servant in this way:

> *He will not cry aloud or lift up his voice, or make it heard in the street; a bruised reed he will not break, and a faintly burning wick he will not quench; he will faithfully bring forth justice. He will not grow faint or be discouraged*
>
> (ISAIAH 42:2–4).

A quiet bishop. A little hobbit. A Messiah who does not shout. When we turn worship upside down, and we plan for service to those in great need, there may be a place for the grand stuff. But let's focus on the quiet things, the little things, the acts that keep helping others when the lightning and thunder are long forgotten.

principle #2
We Want Big Changes,
Not Big Numbers

"And when he came to the house, he allowed no one to enter with him, except Peter and John and James, and the father and mother of the child" (LUKE 8:51).

"Further, take heed that you faithfully perform the business you have to do in the world, from a regard to the commands of God; and not from an ambitious desire of being esteemed better than others."

—DAVID BRAINERD

Getting Mugged in Youth Group

*M*y sons grew up in the Lower East Side when drug dealers stood on the corners and buildings on many blocks were abandoned. We still joke about their youth group at our mission. At some stages, it was a tough group. I was so happy that one time one of my son's best friends from school came to our youth group. Unfortunately, the first time he came he got roughed up. Another teenager took his wallet. I only found out about this a long time later, but my son's friend, understandably, never came back. We also had some youth trips where some of the youth got arrested for shoplifting on the trip. Most of our experiences with the youth were wonderful, but we had some tough days.

In the early days of the mission, what we presented seemed particularly alien to the young people. They just couldn't comprehend it. The inner-city and drug-economy ethos just seemed so strong. I would guess that about 1 teenager a year accepted the Lord and got baptized, and we were thankful for that one.

But God has His own ways, and sea changes affected our neighborhood. The major drug dealer and employer in our area got arrested, and the charges stuck. His trusted co-workers also got picked up. Teenagers started seeing things differently. In the two years after the major bust, about 70 teenagers accepted the Lord. This turn started affecting the whole neighborhood. We would keep saying that it only takes a few geese to change the direction of an entire flock. It took years for these changes to even start, and the change can't be measured by a few numbers.

One of my sons is now starting a ministry in a new neighborhood in New York City. This neighborhood has some of the toughest challenges around. My son has seen enough of the city and God's work and also enough of changing denominational emphases to have a certain amount of wisdom beyond his years. As he looks at the different expectations people have for him, he has made this observation: "Not big numbers, big changes."

It is big changes we are looking for. I cannot quantify in an effective way the changes that have occurred in one of my co-workers. I've known him for more than 25 years. In a group that is trustworthy, he is open about his struggles with crack. I remember ups and downs through the years, victories, and great disappointments. I remember times he spoke in our church, and times he had to go to drug rehab. His story of God's work was not always clear cut, and you couldn't write it in a paragraph.

But as I watch him now, free of drugs and helping mend the neighborhood, I know he is a miracle. His life has shown a big change, but to be honest, he has been around for so long, that people rarely stop to realize what has happened. As I watch him share a joke and encourage a young man, who is at a fork in the road in his life, I know I could never quantify with numbers what God has done through him. *Big changes, but not big numbers.*

The city itself is filled with overwhelming numbers — the number of crimes that occur, the number of children who are underfed, the number of families that are homeless, the number of people looking for work. Numb-ers can get pretty numb-ing, especially if you are one of those numbers. The city itself can seem like a vast machine, and if you are in need, you feel like one tiny number in its huge computation. When we feel less than human, we start acting less than human. That is why in ministry we say, "The bigger the city, the more personal we must become." Little is more powerful than remembering someone's name, someone who has been shuffled from line to line across a series of agencies. When a person feels as though he is something more than a number to you, the possibility for change begins.

Some people in ministry can see the forest, but they are not as good at seeing the individual tree. This is OK, unless you are an individual tree. A ministry can make a person feel like a number just like all the other agencies in the city. Our approach can feel like one more system. Missions teams have different philosophies, but we never *require* someone to hear the gospel in order to receive services. We don't want some-one to feel as though they have one more "system" they have to work in order to get something they need. However, we usually structure a way to *offer* to share the good news we have experienced. I think that this shift in the system makes people feel less like a number or a target, and more like a person.

Bless the Many, Invest in the Few

*I*n ministry, the big numbers will sometimes give the best report, but the big changes are what affect the neighborhood. I thought about this again after Hurricane Sandy hit our area in 2012. Our church was flooded, along with many buildings in our neighborhood. Many resources were used to provide thousands of essential meals in the first weeks. But Graffiti mission chose a different path, helping carry out debris bit by bit with our neighbors in the ravaged buildings around us. We don't have thousands of numbers to report. Little by little with a lot of help, we were able to coordinate a phenomenal amount of work, but it didn't all happen in the first month, and as I write it is still going on.

Still, I think of the people we got to spend time with day by day. One person's husband died after the hurricane—she asked us to help with the funeral because we had been a part of her life in the cleanup. Another is reading the New Testament and asking herself the hard questions because a work team helped her with flooring and gave her a Bible. Another flood victim started helping us do other kinds of ministry at our site.

One person was part of the club stripper scene in Lower Manhattan, and she was helped by another team. She was accepted, even though her dress was different. "This is what the church should be about," she said thoughtfully to one of the hurricane workers, as she flipped some brightly dyed hair out of her eyes. How will anyone be able to quantify what God may be doing in her life? And when?

At one point in our mission, I had a shock. I was meeting to pray with our servant deacons, and I just looked around the room. The servant deacons had been honest about the way God had radically forgiven them and changed their lives. I realized that a majority of the men in the room, by their own public admission, had been either murderers or drug dealers in their earlier lives. They were there to pray, but in another context you wouldn't want to mess with them. They had been a tough bunch. I realized that the process had been so slow that I would never have thought to quantify what God has already done.

Three people were especially important to Jesus. Even though Jesus fed the thousands, He focused on the three. We see Him call them in Luke 5:10. They are with Him at the healing of Jairus's daughter. They are with Him at the Transfiguration. At His toughest moment before He was arrested, He knew the ones He wanted with Him. One of our friends who works for a group that focuses on discipleship will often say, "We aim to bless the many, invest in the few."

We can't be formulaic with Jesus. There were certainly times that He blessed the many, healing and feeding people in the crowds. But clearly being with the Twelve was important to Him, or spending time with Mary and Martha and Lazarus. Sometimes He wanted to be with just the three — Peter, James, and John. That time was not a time for big numbers.

We all want to be practical with our time management. But to be honest, there are times when it seems as though Jesus invested in the wrong people. Jesus had His vulnerable times. He asked the three to stay with Him because He was so sorrowful (Mark 14:40). Yet they failed Him. Later when the tough time comes, the three apparently fled with everyone else (Mark 14:50). So much for investing in the few.

Still, Jesus does it. We have been emphasizing that one of the hardest things to do in life is to judge success. How do you do it? And by what standard? And most importantly, when? If you judged Jesus' methodology on the night when He was arrested, He doesn't seem so successful. His followers all bailed on Him. One follower was the one who deceitfully turned Him in, and one of His special three made a bold-faced denial at the moment of pressure.

How do we judge the success of our own life, and by what standard, and when? One person speaks to thousands, but has little real influence. Another person says the kind word to one person at the right time, and that person influences the world. One person makes millions of dollars and is well-known but dies in a self-centered cocoon. Another dies with very little, and no one really remembers the vast influence wielded by him on the lives of those who survived him. That's just the way it goes.

What happened to the three who were such total failures when the great test came? Their lives continued, and they became lessons. Acts 12 catches us up on two of them. One of them dies by the hand of oppression, and one of them escapes prison, but no one bewails as a failure the one who died. James is apparently the first of the Twelve to die. His death is a valuable lesson for the new group. Clearly, death is not the end of things, and value is seen beyond the boundaries of a long life or a quiet demise.

The lesson that the death of James brings to the church is the importance of context. Without an appropriate context, his death seems so untimely. Perhaps the most important thing for us to do is to put an event in an appropriate context.

A while ago I read the story of a train in Indiana. A train was moving at about 20 miles an hour along a track. You might think that speed was fairly slow unless you thought about how much it took to stop a 6,000-ton train. As the conductor looked ahead, he thought he saw a dog on the track. But what he thought was a dog lifted its head, and he realized that it was really a small child. The child was only 19 months old and had wandered away as the mother had worked in a garden nearby.

The engineer blew the whistle and put on the brake. The child looked up but did not move. By now the train had slowed to 10 miles an hour, but that speed was still too fast. The conductor, a Vietnam veteran, climbed out on the railing of the engine. He scrambled to the front of the train. Slowly, ever so slowly, the small child began to move off the track. She was not fast enough. As the train came upon her, her body was right over the rail. The conductor stretched out his foot and somehow was able to gently kick the child off the track, so that she tumbled down the ground declining away from the track. Her only injuries were some scratches and a chipped tooth.

Later, the conductor was hailed as a hero. But the story made me think again about context. What if someone had only told the mother that a man had kicked her child and that the child had incurred a cracked tooth and some cuts? Probably the mother would be furious. But if someone explained the larger story, she might have been quite grateful for this special care given to her child, and felt perhaps a bit ashamed. In the same way, without a context of eternity and all that had happened before, James's death could seem incomprehensible. But in the context of eternity, we find another way to look at things. James helps us see how the church deals with the unfair death of one of the Twelve. Without James, one of the three, and without his example in the church, we might face unreasonable death with a different attitude.

In the same chapter, Peter is actually freed from prison. Yet in his testimony in the Gospels, he doesn't seem to hesitate to remind people of *his* own failure. Eventually, he is the source of two letters called by his name. By tradition, he was the companion of Mark, who, according to scholars, wrote the first Gospel. It seems as though Matthew and Luke referred to Mark's Gospel as they wrote their versions. Then we also know that when Christ appeared to Paul, Paul made sure to go and spend 15 days with Peter, one of the Jesus' Three (Galatians 1:18). Paul eventually wrote a lot of the letters in the New Testament. So, in a lot of ways, without Peter, several of the Gospels and some of the letters would not have been written the way they were.

Then we come to John, the other one of the three. By tradition, John the Apostle was the source of the Gospel of John, the three letters of John, and Revelation. So one might ask, what would the New Testament look like without those three, who seemed to be such complete failures at one point? At that point of failure, the numbers just didn't look that good. Some might have challenged Jesus for just spending time with three people. It all depends on when we evaluate things.

Kicked Out of Yale

Some things are easy to evaluate. If you want to see if you are improving in your weight-lifting program, you can simply check the pounds of your weight and the number of repetitions. Clearly, other things are harder. For example, our generation has struggled to evaluate the quality of our nation's education. Does a standardized test fulfill our need to adequately judge? Can the tests evaluate perseverance, character, intuitive moments, joy in learning, creative solutions after a long period of time, or original thinking? We do the best we can, but realize we are often woefully unable to be confident in the numbers we present. The complexity of how a mind works and how things are actually accomplished escapes us.

The challenge of judging is no new issue. In Charles Dickens's *Hard Times*, the educator Thomas Gradgrind is a great characterization of "a man of facts and calculations." He is confident that if he trains his students to look at the world from the lens of his statistics and objective realities, he has educated them successfully. As the story proceeds, however, we gradually realize how wrong his confidence is. In the end, even though his numbers proclaim success, the reader realizes what an extreme failure his methods turn out to be. For this man of facts, life turned out to be a lot more than he had imagined.

On an even deeper level, how does one evaluate something like "the enlargement of the kingdom of God"? I am currently rereading the diary of a missionary who seemed like a failure in terms of his numbers as he continued his ministry. He was expelled from Yale, and repeatedly requested reinstatement, but was refused. Because of his expulsion, his options for ministry were drastically reduced, but he eventually was commissioned as a missionary to Native Americans in his area in the Northeast of our country. His health was deteriorating and from his journal, he seemed to me to be suffering from deep depression.

Despite his hard work, his first assignment for missions work produced no tangible results. The Native Americans in that area were understandably hostile to Christianity and another view laced with drunkenness prevailed in the tribe. He was reassigned and his second place of ministry also produced very little.

This young man's name was David Brainerd. He continued to pray and write in his journal, despite his feelings of melancholy and his health challenges. At this point in his life, the numbers for his evangelistic efforts were abysmal. In reviewing his performance, one might think that given his track record, his future prospects seemed weak.

However, something happened at his third place of ministry that seemed inexplicable from our normal view. As he preached to his beloved "Indians," he felt a "sweet" presence of God. People listening in his little group of listeners began to weep quietly. Some began to beg to come to Christ. More came to listen. The behavior of the whole community took on a remarkable change. He saw real transformation in Christ. Where he received only mockery before, people lined up to participate and be baptized.

Yet how can one evaluate his life? David Brainerd died at the age of 29. He had become sicker and sicker, and his journal entries had become fewer and fewer. From one standpoint, even at the end of his life, the actual numbers of the conversions in his ministry were relatively small. However, Brainerd died in the home of his mentor—the brilliant theologian Jonathan Edwards, who was so important in the Great Awakening going on at that time.

Edwards compiled and edited Brainerd's diary, which was published over and over again, and has inspired people of prayer and missionaries up to the present time. Extremely influential missionaries and preachers such as John Wesley, William Carey, Adoniram Judson, and Jim Elliot were all deeply affected by Brainerd's life and journal. What if someone evaluated his life at the end of his first two failed ministries, or even at the end of his life? Now, more than two and one-half centuries later, we see some of the results of his short life. Once one thinks about it, we may not know all of the results of any life, with the vagaries of our little existence, until the last ticking of the clock, and the last spinning of the galaxies. But then, David Brainerd was clearly after something more than numbers.

principle #3
It's About Seeing, Not Hearing

"Go and tell John what you have seen and heard: the blind receive their sight, the lame walk, lepers are cleansed, and the deaf hear, the dead are raised up, the poor have good news preached to them" (LUKE 7:22, JESUS).

"I find that to be a fool as to worldly wisdom, and to commit my cause to God, not fearing to offend men, who take offence at the simplicity of truth, is the only way to remain unmoved at the sentiments of others."

—JOHN WOOLMAN

Anything for a Quarter

*I*t was the greatest sermon ever preached in our mission and I never said a word. Jackie was famous in our neighborhood. I had known him since I first arrived in the Lower East Side. He was slightly built, talkative, and friendly. He lived in the park. He wasn't abusive or violent. He was an alcoholic. Everyone knew him.

Jackie would drift in and out of some of our missions work from time to time. Sometimes he would come to our meal. He was willing to talk about anything. We talked about God, drinking, surviving in New York City, the Bible, and on and on.

Things usually don't stay the same for anybody. Jackie's situation seemed to deteriorate. I began to see Jackie more and more on the sidewalks, pleading with friends or strangers for money.

Memory is so funny. We forget so many things that should be important, and then a few tiny moments stand out in vivid clarity. I remember a defining moment with Jackie. It was a rainy day and I was in a place in my own work where I was depressed, tired, and discouraged. I had finished a long and frustrating day at the mission, and I knew my wife, Susan, and our kids were waiting on me. All I wanted to do was to get out of that storefront and go home.

I exited from the door and there was Jackie, rumpled, wet, with a pleading look on his face. Drips of water were running down his face. "Please," he begged, "just give me a quarter, that's all I ask, just give me a quarter."

Two emotions leaped up inside of me like frazzled old dogs. On the one hand, we don't give out money because we find that we tend to just participate in the addict's problem. Jackie knew that. One emotion was that I just wanted to leave him and go home.

On the other hand, his pathetic situation broke my heart, and I wanted to give him some money. I felt so sorry for him, so sorry that alcohol had led him to become something less than human, a begging machine, thinking only of the next quarter.

"I am not going to give you any money, Jackie, you know that. I can give you something to eat if you want, but no money."

"Please," he whined, "please, just a quarter, please."

I refused. I began to walk away, and then I turned around. The drizzle turned into a downpour. Jackie sat down on a concrete block in the front of our building, and leaned over with his head in his hands. Then he began to vomit. The rain washed the vomit across the sidewalk into the gutter.

I stood and looked at him for a while as we both stood in the storm. I must confess, as I looked at him, I thought, *This man will never change. He is hopeless.* Then I turned and walked away, feeling as though the two dogs within me were shredding my insides. I would have felt guilty if I gave him the only thing he wanted, money, and I felt guilty walking away.

For a number of years, that memory was connected to a low point in my work here, at least for me. But stories have a way of continuing after we have put a marker to end them.

Several years later I was surprised to learn that Jackie had actually volunteered to go to our recovery program outside the city. I had come to learn the hard way that out of 500 people on the street who would say that they want a recovery program, only about 1 person would actually go. At least those were my personal statistics. I was fascinated with human nature. Some who knew they needed help the most would get close to going. Then they would say they needed to take care of their dog, or something had come up with their girlfriend, or their mother had gotten sick. They wouldn't go.

But Jackie turned out to be the 1 in 500. He cleaned up. He went to the Bible study provided each day at the recovery site. His faith in Christ became something living. He did his work assignments. He breathed in the fresh country air. He went to the local Alcoholics Anonymous meetings. He talked a lot with the leader of the group. He built up a track record. He did manual labor on the land. He got a job in the area outside the program. He bought a pickup truck, a remarkable achievement for someone who had lived on the streets for so long.

Finally one day he came back to our mission to visit. He came on a Wednesday night, the night we had a meal for anyone who wanted one in our area. The storefront was filled with people who lived on the edge of society, dwelling in abandoned buildings and on the street. It was always a bit raucous.

Jackie opened the door. He was standing straight up for once. He looked me straight in the eye and smiled. I was shocked at how healthy he looked. His grin was contagious. A silence began to spread across the room, until there were only a few people talking. That silence was so unusual that the few people left talking got silent too.

"Jackie?" someone said. "No, it can't be. Is that Jackie?" Murmurs rippled through the group. Then the room was filled with shouting and greeting, mixed with disbelief. Jackie had people's total attention. I didn't have to say a word.

Finally I said, "Jackie is going to stay for Bible study." For once in my life, I didn't have to try to convince or beg anyone to stay. No one drifted away without making eye contact with me. The place was packed. Jackie spoke about what God had done in simple words. He didn't have deep theological training or any rhetorical skill. Yet the group of grizzled street people hung on his every word.

His was the best sermon ever preached at our mission, and I hadn't said anything. The truth underneath Jackie's experience is so obvious that we have to hear it again every few decades. We had no slick packaging, no wise marketer to help us make the message more user-friendly. The draw was in the result.

A wise, new pastor in Queens recently said it clearly. He had learned from experience in his neighborhood that often people can't *hear* the gospel unless they *see* the gospel. My friends on Seventh Street saw the gospel when Jackie walked in the door. Then the Holy Spirit opened their hearts to hear the gospel shared in the simplest of ways.

In Jail and Discouraged

*L*ike I said, this realization of the visible evidence of the gospel is nothing new. Since I have been around a while, I have watched different church traditions swing back and forth concerning different truths. Some traditions see groups of people that stress out doing the tangible so much and so hard that they lose the inner power of the good news. Their "social gospel," or whatever lingo they use, becomes eventually mostly social with little good news. Then another group focuses on the spoken word so much and rejects anything that smacks of social work, so much so that the power of the tangible work is forgotten. Then, of course, a group rediscovers the power of getting our hands dirty with real people in messy situations and promotes it again. And on and on.

I have seen the pendulum a lot. Of course, it is not a strict pendulum, perhaps it is a circle or some other kind of continuum. Whatever it is, sometimes our spiritual journey is a journey of rediscovering truths at the heart of life, truths we have really known all along.

Once again I think of my friend, a Christian leader who grew up in the Bronx, whom I mentioned in the introduction. He would comment on the most recent denominational fad or Christian movement that people get so excited about. "This is not new," he would say, "it is just new to you."

I am fascinated by a story in the Bible about a man who was apparently pretty discouraged about the Messiah. His name was John the Baptist and he had reason to be discouraged. He proclaimed the Messiah, a person that John expected would make things right in the world. Perhaps John expected the Messiah to confront the immorality in the royalty and the leaders of the nation so that the entire nation would rise up and change. Instead, John found himself thrown in prison. The circumstances simply didn't seem to match what he was proclaiming. In Luke 7:19, he sends some followers to Jesus and he has them ask Jesus a question. "Are you the one who is to come, or shall we look for another?"

Jesus' response is revealing. He doesn't condemn John for his doubt. Neither does He give him a doctrinal answer, defining some intellectual essence of messiahship. He simply tells John to see what is happening. People are getting healed. The blind are seeing and the lame are walking. Good news, really good news, is being preached not so much to the rich and influential, those on a fast-track career, but to the poor. People can see that something is happening, as well as hear it (Luke 7:22).

The Odd Christian with the Weird Clothes

*I*f we only learn from people who agree with us on everything, we will have a pretty narrow ability to learn. I don't even agree with my wife on everything, and I would be a poor learner if I blocked all I have learned from her. In a sense, I think as we mature in our walk with Christ, we are able to appreciate others who are on the same walk but are quite different from us. It doesn't mean we have to give up who we are to appreciate another person on the road. It's a big kingdom, after all.

I have been reading again the journal of an American in the eighteenth century, a man that many thought of at that time as somewhat odd. He was part of the Quaker movement, which at that time was committed to the Bible and the leadings of the Holy Spirit based on the Bible. He was an industrious, thoughtful, and practical person.

Perhaps one of his most profound insights into the American culture of his own day was that the inordinate love of luxury pulled people into many social ills that they were not even aware of. This surge toward inappropriate prosperity led to hurry, disordered work, slavery, and abuse of people involved in trade. This was hundreds of years ago in America. I wonder what he would say now.

Some Quakers at that time were slave owners, and they didn't see any discrepancy between their belief and their actions. They had many ways of justifying what they did. Even if they treated their slaves relatively well, and some of them did, they did not really think deeply about the dynamics of the slave trade and what they had done to the people that were bought and sold like property.

John Woolman had his own way of addressing the problem. He would wait in a Quaker meeting and pray, and only speak when he felt the Spirit's direct leading to speak. Sometimes he was silent for a long time. But when he spoke, he prayed his words would speak like a trumpet concerning what was important in the way Quakers were actually living.

Yet he would not only speak. At his own expense, he would travel to other Quakers and stay with them. When he headed south, he said he felt "a dark gloominess hanging over the land." Sometimes he visited Quakers who had slaves and he gently refused to sleep in their houses. He did not want to profit in any way from what slaves did. Often he would quietly speak directly to the slave owner in private. In his journal, he would say that these direct conversations were not easy to do. Some of these Quakers were wealthy, older, and well respected in their community. Still, he persisted in his own calm way. He wanted his own life to be consistent with his walk with Christ.

He knew that the dye for clothes came from indigo, which was a product of the slave trade. He decided that he would not wear clothing with dye in it. To be honest, this behavior made him appear rather odd to many people—the weird-looking clothes probably didn't help. In addition, as a businessman he stopped retailing rum, sugar, and molasses because they were a part of the slave trade. He had a lot of explaining to do with his customers when he wouldn't sell these things. To identify with slaves, he refused to ride a horse and would only travel by walking.

As odd as he appeared sometimes, people began to see the love of the gospel in what he did rather than in just what he said. He persisted for a long time. He refused to take the aggressive tactics of some other people at the time because he felt he was not led by the Spirit to do so. People around him didn't just hear what they shouldn't do, but rather they saw the good news in this man who took a consistent and gentle stand for the love of others. Thanks in great part to his efforts, by 1787 it is claimed that no American Quaker owned slaves. In his own life, he helped people to see the gospel in a different way, so that eventually they were able to hear the transforming gospel for our country.

Clearly this kind of gospel sharing works itself out in so many different ways. A group of young people in Manhattan call themselves "travelers." They move from place to place, often have dogs with them, and many times take a stance against any perceived authority, including religious authority. I remember one who was a self-proclaimed atheist. He watched what our mission did after Hurricane Sandy. We put a generator outside so people could recharge their phones. We provided food on the street. Work teams rallied to clean out our own church and then the buildings around us. He asked in frustration, "How come atheists aren't doing cool things like this?" We saw once again how simple kindness can transcend so many barriers.

Reading again the primary writings, the Word of God helps us remember that you can't really dissect the gospel. Jesus didn't wake up with His disciples in the morning and say, "Today we're going to do the evangelism gospel, or the church planting gospel, or the social gospel, or the discipleship gospel." It was always simply the gospel. The gospel is so expansive, it touches everything. If we look, we can almost always hear/see/touch the good news, whether we are dealing with salvation or sewage, heaven or housing, preaching or peanut butter sandwiches.

principle #4
We Want Hardening, Not Softening

"Brace yourself like a man" (Job 38:3 NIV, God to Job).

"But you oughtta thank me before I die for the gravel in your guts and the spit in your eye."

—Shel Silverstein

More Tenacity than Talent

We were in the middle of a big ministry operation at a critical time in San Francisco. Thousands of people were being fed each day. The lines reached around the block. Hundreds of people were getting jobs through our work. We knew we were doing something we thought was important, but discouraging things would happen. We felt burned out. Finally, we had some people come in to train our workers. I don't remember much of anything about the training anymore — only the compassionate look on the man's face.

We were all crowded almost shoulder to shoulder in the hot room. Someone shared a discouraging story about a time she wanted to help a person but had to say no. The trainer smiled gently. He said, "My mother worked to help others in this city for more than 50 years. She would sometimes say to me the following words, which were hard for me to hear, 'Son, sometimes you have to harden your heart in order to serve.'"

I know that compassion is the heart of why we work to help someone else, and I know that some overworked and frustrated people involved in tangible ministries have become cynical and as mean as snakes. Yet there is a certain kind of toughening that has to happen if we are to be truly devoted. We will encounter hurt feelings and discouragements and defeats, and it would be easy to simply bail when the first disappointments come.

So around the heart of compassion, I am always looking for toughness to develop, an unwillingness to quit; a bulldog steadfastness that is going to keep on, no matter what. In a lot of areas of service, I think tenacity is a lot more important than talent.

My wife sometimes gives women this spiritual direction, "If you are tired of starting over, stop giving up." There may be times when God tells you to quit or leave a situation. But there are also times when we are to stay and "harden our heart"—toughen up a bit.

When someone asks me what qualities I am looking for concerning someone to work to express Christ in tangible ways, the first thing I say is often this, "We need someone with tough skin."

The Impatience of Job

Job is a book in the Bible that you can go back to again and again and find something different each time. Recently I read the book again, and I was struck more by the *persevering* "impatience of Job" rather than the "patience of Job." "As for me, is my complaint against man? Why should I not be impatient?" he even asks (21:4). Job complains, laments, and demands from God to explain how Job is unrighteous and how on earth God is righteous.

Finally, after 37 chapters, God appears. In a sense, God blows Job's mind. He kind of retreads his brain. He does a hard reset on all his perceptions. God blows Job's fuses. He shifts everything into overdrive. God appears as a tornado.

I watched a tornado form once when I was plowing in Oklahoma. It was one of the eeriest, most otherworldly things in nature I have ever seen. The whirlwind almost looked like a cartoon, moving across the land, its funnel growing darker and darker. I didn't really believe in God at the time, but I began to pray. I prayed that the whirlwind or tornado or whatever it was would not come toward me but would go away from me.

So the whirlwind came to Job and his friends. In our time, we would compare the sound of a tornado to that of a freight train. I wonder what Job and his friends thought it sounded like. This is where I need to stop for a moment. Everything in me would say in the story, it is time for God to come with loving arms open for Job and ready to answer his urgent questions. According to my view, God needs to say something like, "I hear your pain," and give him some tender-loving care after all of Job's many chapters of lamenting and arguing.

I didn't really understand what God was doing until I remembered how I wrestled with my own boys. When my sons were about six and eight years old, I would wrestle with them. Sure, I could beat them. I could crush them. I weighed about four times as much as they did. I could break their arms if I had wanted to. But it wasn't that kind of wrestling. This was another kind of wrestling. This kind of wrestling meant getting on my hands and knees and giving them a chance to push against me. And I would push against them, testing their ability, strengthening their muscles by pushing back.

Now I thought, *which type of father is the better father?* One father, knowing his power and his responsibilities, says, "I wouldn't think of wrestling with you. If I really wrestled, I would hurt you. I have far more important things to do."

But the other kind of father gets down on all fours, gives a push to one of his sons, and says, "Let's see what you got, big guy."

What kind of father does a little boy really want? He wants the kind of father who will engage him, tussle with him, give him a little pushback, take him seriously.

Once I think about things in this way, I see it all the time in the Bible, and all the time in life. God is merciful. But God gives Abraham a chance to plead for the city in Genesis 18. God tells Jacob he has wrestled with God in Genesis 32. God, who is gracious, gives Moses the chance to plead for his people in Exodus 32. Of course, God is kind and compassionate. But He is also seeing what His children are made of.

Jesus did the same thing for those that came to Him. When the Canaanite woman asked for help, Jesus says something that some people might consider racist or abusive. "It is not right to take the children's bread and throw it to the dogs" (Matthew 15:26). If she had been thin-skinned, she could have walked away and never come back. But she was tough, and she pressed for what Luther called "the deep hidden yes under the no." You can't help but like her. With her spunky answer, Jesus tells her that her faith is great.

Put on Your Big Boy Pants

Through Christ, we are called the children of Israel. The word *Israel* means "one who strives with God." So when God comes to Job in this moment of great encounter, does He say some words of comfort, like He does so many times in the Bible? No, it is almost as if God gets down on His hands and knees and says, "Job, you have been asking and complaining and lamenting and challenging My rightness, now let's see what you are made of." At the beginning of both of God's speeches, He says the same thing. Literally, it means "gird up your loins like a man" (38:3; 40:7). This was the ancient way of telling people to tuck in their robe to get ready to work, or, well, wrestle.

My translation for "gird up your loins like a man" is "put on your big boy pants."

In the end, maybe it is only God who can say such a thing to us. Like Job's friends, we are so quick to advise about what someone who is suffering should do. But sooner or later, a person has to face the statement, "I'm sorry that your spouse left you, I am sorry that this co-worker made you lose your job, I'm sorry that you had a heart murmur as a child, I'm sorry your father was never there, I'm sorry you have feelings of inferiority, I'm sorry that your mother was abusive, but you can't let that fact control the rest of your life. It is time to put on your big boy pants (or your big girl pants)."

It is the same way with upside-down devotion that shows itself in service. People with their frailties and demands will discourage us tremendously. However, sometimes we have to harden our hearts, put on our big boy pants, and keep serving.

God was not through with His tussle with Job. Job had asked a lot of questions for God. God didn't soothe Job and give him the explanations after all of Job's questions. After telling Job to buck up, God asked questions of His own. A lot of them. I didn't count them, but I've read that He asked 77 questions. It's almost as if He gave Job a bit of pushback.

Yet His questions helped Job come to a different understanding of the world—God's questions point to beauty and wonder and complexity in the cosmos, in the weather, in the biosphere. God finally asked Job to consider two creatures, the behemoth and the leviathan. They are a strange pair to conclude with, if you are talking about the wonder of the universe. The descriptions of the two animals sound like a hippopotamus and a crocodile. God points to a lot of qualities in these beasts, but both of His descriptions point to the fact that these two creatures have a special quality. They are tough.

The hippo creature refuses to let turbulence get to him. "Behold, if the river is turbulent he is not frightened; he is confident though Jordan rushes against his mouth" (40:23). God gives a great description of being thick-skinned when he speaks of the crocodile creature: "The folds of his flesh stick together, firmly cast on him and immovable. . . . Though the sword reaches him, it does not avail. . . . For him sling stones are turned to stubble. . . . He laughs at the rattle of javelins" (41:23, 26, 28, 29). Astonishingly, that's how God ends his entire talk with Job, pointing with admiration to these tough turbo-beasts.

Job does a lot of lamenting and challenging and demanding in this book, yet somehow he presses on and refuses to quit when his friends' formulaic, question-free theology doesn't match his experience. In fact, God told the friends that they didn't speak right about Him as His servant Job did. Personally, I think God kind of liked Job's spunk.

Growing Up with Some Gravel in Your Gut

*W*e have done a great disservice to the word *calloused*. We call a person who is insensitive to the needs of other people, cynical about life, a calloused person. But we have forgotten how valuable calluses really are. Calluses are what help a person work. Calluses on the hands help people function without having their hands shredded by hard use. We couldn't do a lot of things without calluses. Without calluses on certain parts of the heart, I think a person might implode with the suffering. Think of a person who works in an emergency room or with crowds of homeless people. In times of critical need, there may not be time for the luxury of reflective tenderness, nor would it be appropriate.

We all know this innately. Johnny Cash sang about a boy with a terrible name who got toughened up as he grew up. By having a little gravel in his gut and spit in his eye, Shel Silverstein says, he was able to try and win.

Sometimes when we are an advocate for someone who can't plea for themselves, we have to be tough. One of the ways a bureaucracy in a big city wins is by shuffling the caller to another department, or by wearing the caller down by delay tactics. This is the time for that bulldog tenacity, that endurance, that Christians are so famous for. We know that you can't just leave a message and wait and wait for a callback. Or if the email didn't work, we find another way. In trying to get answers from a large city government or corporate organization, many people just give up. In my experience advocating for others, I have found it helpful to always keep a record of the time and the name of every contact I have made. As the number of calls pile up, I will respectfully remind the person of the number of calls I have made, the dates, and the people I have talked to. This little action helps encourage people that they are being held accountable. Letting a person or organization know you are not giving up can work wonders.

We are not going to avoid the tough times anyway. When I taught in the East, I would hear the story of Buddha's father. Buddha's father didn't want his son to ever experience suffering or even see suffering, and he was rich and powerful enough to accomplish this kind of protection for a while. Eventually Buddha left the palace and saw for the first time an old man, a diseased man, and a corpse. Even the young, protected Buddha had to deal with aging, with health challenges, and with death, just like everyone else. A parent naturally wants to shield the child from all suffering, but in the end, that isn't really good for the child. It's probably not good for us either.

While I was reading Job, I remembered an incident that happened to me many decades ago. When I was five years old, a certain TV channel was showing a Saturday afternoon movie. It was *The Mummy* with Boris Karloff. I'm sure it would seem mild now, but I shouldn't have seen it. I don't know where the rest of the family was. I was all alone in the living room, and I was transfixed. The mummy was painfully slow moving—you'd think anyone could run away from him. But he was so creepy, always sneaking up on people who were so agonizingly unaware. After the movie was over, I was terrified, and could hardly pass a closet.

That night, my mom tried to comfort me by reading a story book to me. It was about a little boy. Guess what the little boy called his mother? Mummy. I begged my mom not to read anymore.

My mother told me I could stay home from kindergarten on Monday, but I would have to go on Tuesday. I remember what it felt like to walk those few blocks to kindergarten all on my own that next Tuesday. The sidewalk seemed endless and passed all kinds of dark doors. Now I understand a bit more about what my mom must have felt like, watching her little five-year-old walk down the street, even though everything in her wanted to comfort me and let me stay home. I had to put on my big boy pants.

Passing On Opportunities to Give Up

For me, Jesus of Nazareth is the heart of compassion. But I have observed that in one sense, every time He chose mercy and inclusion of others, there was also a rejection. His choice to be a friend of sinners, as the charge went, was also a rebuttal of those who cultivated a different moral palate. The kind of people who most people want to please hated Him for these choices. Jesus often had to harden His heart to one thing in order to follow the call to serve.

It is fascinating for me to see how He consistently determined to pass by opportunities to be discouraged. He hardened His heart to disappointment. In my opinion, there are always a thousand reasons to quit when you are serving others. Jesus' experience with the three siblings at Bethany in John 11 is an example. Jesus had about six opportunities to quit, and He decided to pass them by. I think you and I will have the same kind of opportunities to stop.

One opportunity to stop serving will be when people try to put you on their schedule. We will never have enough time to do everything other people want us to do. When Mary and Martha sent for Jesus and told Him that Lazarus was ill, they surely wanted Him to come right away. But the Bible says that Jesus stayed two days longer where He was (vv. 3–6). When Jesus finally gets to Bethany, both sisters, at separate times, remind Him that His timing is way off (vv. 21, 32). Jesus could have just thrown up His hands and said, "That's it, I quit! Everyone is trying to tell Me what to do and when. I can't take it anymore. What about time for Me?" I'm glad He didn't go that route.

A second opportunity to stop serving will be when people dislike you. I find no promise in the Bible that when you help the poor or afflicted they will be grateful. On the streets of New York, I have heard some vividly graphic ways to curse, sometimes directed at me. One time was when we were working to convert a handout program to a work program. One of the recipients was so incensed at the change that every time he saw me for about two years he followed behind me and cursed me out. Sometimes for blocks. A college student who came here to work as a summer missionary a long time ago had grown up in a somewhat protected environment. At the end of the summer, during debriefing, she was asked what she had learned during the summer. She simply said, "I've learned that MF doesn't stand for Mission Friends."

But to be honest, words are just words. I have only been threatened with skull-crushing stones one time. We were in a tent city on a vacant lot, and a camera crew was following someone who was working at Graffiti and who lived there. The inhabitants had said we could film as long as we filmed only the worker from Graffiti. Despite fair warning, the cameraman kept panning the entire tent city area. After the fourth time he did it, a half brick whizzed past my head. Then another. We saw a rain of bricks coming our way. I have never seen a camera crew move so fast.

When Jesus told His followers that they were going back to Judea, they started thinking about heavy projectiles that break bones. "Rabbi, the Jews were just now seeking to stone you, and are you going there again?" (v. 8). Jesus could have said,

"I don't have to go to a place where people treat Me like that. I've got to have some self-respect." I'm glad He kept going.

The third opportunity we will have to quit serving is when our own friends misunderstand us. I have often heard certain workers say, "I can understand when non-Christians don't understand, but it's the Christians who say wrong things about us that drive me nuts." It isn't the first time. Jesus' disciples in this story don't really get it. When Jesus speaks metaphorically about death, they think Jesus is saying that Lazarus is only sleeping. When they finally follow Him, they think they are walking into a stoning trap and are about to die (v. 16). Once again, they are wrong. Jesus could have quit for the same reason that other Christians have when people from their own faith perspective don't understand them. I'm glad He didn't.

The fourth opportunity for us to quit is one that comes repeatedly. It is when people tell you what you should have done. This kind of challenge has a cumulative effect. It's when people tell you what you should have done retrospectively, and they tell you so repeatedly, that it begins to get to you. Sometimes they are armchair quarterbacks, spouting off easy perceptions from their seat rather than on the field. Sometimes they are victims of real difficulty and they have true observations about another way you could have done things. Either way, it is still tough to hear. In this story, for example, there are three different times when people say what Jesus should have done. Martha says, in effect, that if Jesus had come earlier, He could have fixed things (v. 21). Mary, a little later, says the same thing (v. 32). In the middle of Jesus' own grieving, the people in general say the same thing again—"Could not he who opened the eyes of the blind man also have kept this man from dying?" (v. 37). I could see Jesus walking off in a huff, saying, "That does it, I am tired of everyone saying repeatedly what I should have done. Stop saying that! I need a vacation." I am glad He didn't walk off.

A fifth opportunity for us to quit is when circumstances simply stink. Life is simply messy. I'm not a big fan of messiness. For a little while in my life, when we were on vacation in the mountains, I took up fly-fishing. I loved having my fishing rod in the trunk of my car (in New York I don't even have a car) and going out to stand in some beautiful stream and cast out my line. But I really didn't want to catch anything. If I had caught something, I would have to grapple with pulling the hook out, and then putting the fish in a bucket. I would have to let that fishiness slosh around in my nice rental car, and then go home and face all the messiness of cleaning it on the back patio, and on and on. I just wanted the semblance of fishing, not the real thing. Real fish stink and can mess up the very nice interior of my car trunk.

In the same way, when we work to serve others, things get messy. It got messy for Jesus in this story. Practical Martha has to instruct Jesus that He can't have the stone to the tomb opened because the corpse has been there four days and there will be a stink (11:39). Jesus could have wrinkled up His nose and said, "Well, yuck, no one wants that. Let's do something else. Anyone game for a picnic in a meadow far away from here instead?" But Jesus didn't say that.

The sixth opportunity to quit is often the straw that breaks the back. It happens when we have resisted all the other opportunities to quit and the hard thing is done. The event is over. The ministry has been accomplished. The victory may have even been achieved. You are understandably exhausted. Yet the building still has to be cleaned up. The signs have to be taken down. The forms have to be counted. The tables have to be folded. In the glow of the event, no one is thinking of these things. The others may even go home rejoicing, not thinking, feeling all was done. Yet someone has to do it.

In this story, Jesus does the remarkable. Lazarus is raised from the dead. Victory is achieved. Lazarus walks out. Or rather, he hobbles out. Maybe he has to bunny hop. I don't know. We are told his feet are bound. But no one gets it. You'd think they would have figured it out. Jesus still has to tell the others to do one more thing. He has to tell the people to unbind him, and release him (11:44).

Isn't it funny, how there always seems to be one more thing in service? Even when we plan ahead very well, there often is that one more thing to do beyond the limit of our energy or expectation. If we don't toughen up a bit and become ready for it, those circumstances can sneak up behind us at the end and sap our spirit. Jesus in this story could have been irritated. He could have said, "Do I have to tell you everything? Go ahead and leave poor Lazarus in a cocoon of burial cloths, for all I care. I'm through!" But Jesus passed up that one other opportunity to be discouraged. He had toughened His heart in order to serve.

Guilty Either Way

*T*his kind of toughening is upside-down devotion. Of course we need tender hearts, but I think in reality we need tough *and* tender hearts. A tough and tender heart will help us to really serve.

Addiction is the category of our time. It limits our health, our sanity, or morals, our souls, our lives. David Wilcox, the songwriter, has a wonderful song entitled, "Guilty Either Way." In the song, Wilcox describes a friend addicted to drugs who knocks on his door. Wilcox feels guilty if he gives him money. He feels guilty if he refuses. It feels like a lose-lose situation. We know instinctively that the truly tender heart has to be tough also. Our long-term mercy may limit our short-term response, a short-term response that feels like mercy but really isn't. It is hard to say this statement to someone who is addicted: "I won't help you unless you let me be a part of your life." There always seem to be such easier and simpler ways to help. But in the end these easy ways only cooperate with the problem. This kind of stuff is messy and creates a lot of misunderstanding. It comes with the territory.

Many Christians have "power verses," verses that they go back to again and again for support in difficult times. This is one that helps me when I feel as though my heart is going to crumble, to implode with all the misunderstandings and difficulties. It helps me keep going. It is a song that talks about the man who truly reverences God and delights in His instruction. This man "is not afraid of bad news; his heart is firm, trusting in the LORD. His heart is steady; he will not be afraid, until he looks in triumph on his adversaries" (Psalm 112:7–8).

His heart is tough, established, unwavering. This person has turned a soft devotion upside down. When opportunities to quit arise in service, and they will, his heart will even look, not soft, but hard.

principle #5
It's the Inside Stuff, Not the Outside Stuff

"Which is easier, to say to the paralytic, 'Your sins are forgiven,' or to say, 'Rise, take up your bed and walk'?" (MARK 2:9, JESUS).

"In using all means, seek God alone. In and through every outward thing, look only to the power of His Spirit, and the merits of His Son. Beware you do not get stuck in the work itself; if you do, it is all lost labor."

— JOHN WESLEY, *HOW TO PRAY: THE BEST OF JOHN WESLEY ON PRAYER*

The Plotline from the Inside to the Outside

apoleon once said, "To understand the man you have to know what was happening in the world when he was twenty." I'm at the point in life where I think the conversation starts by understanding what the world was like for the person when that person was a young adult.

In my generation, I clearly remember experiencing anger at those who looked at our society and then blamed the victim. That blaming often had educational overtones, or economic overtones, or racialist overtones. I also remember my impatience with a sickly sweet benevolence that spiritualized hard, real problems in the world. My mind moved in the direction of practical needs. At one point, I decided to be a lawyer, because a lawyer deals with what I saw as "real" needs. So I moved from a childhood seeming to ignore the pressing social needs of our times to a young adulthood seeing all the answers in addressing those specific needs.

But we have continued to change. The change is something different than a political choice. Others have thought about the politics of those changes. Winston Churchill and others have said something like, "If you're not a liberal at twenty, you have no heart. If you're not a conservative at forty, you have no brain." No, the change is different than just a changing political sensibility. The change really involves moving from an outside sensibility to perceiving the inside.

Perhaps an example will help explain this idea. I remember a slogan in our urban area, "Housing is a right." That statement certainly makes sense to me. But it is more and more clear that as important as the outside circumstances are, they are not the critical thing. I watched a crack addict demand and receive housing and ruin it in a matter of months. Housing wasn't really the answer. Something has to happen on the inside of a person. As the old saying went, "It's not so much getting the person out of the ghetto, but it's getting the ghetto out of the person."

Things usually work from the inside out. This truth is so perennial that we forget it. When the religious people wanted Jesus to focus on when the kingdom of God was coming, Jesus said it wouldn't be like that. It won't have outward signs to be observed, He said. We won't be able to say, "Look, here it is!" Jesus said that "the kingdom of God is in the midst of you," or within you, like right now (Luke 17:21).

We see this plotline a lot in the Bible. We repeat the statement concerning Moses. It took one day for God to get the people of God out of Egypt. It took 40 years to get Egypt out of the people of God. It is the inside work that matters. Then the outside work changes. Perhaps this is true of many of the characters in the Bible—Abraham, Joseph, Moses, David. Each one has a period where the circumstances they are in don't match their expectations. It looks as though God is doing the training on the inside. The outside circumstances change later.

John Wesley wrote an evocative statement about the man who was paralyzed in Mark 2. Wesley said that Jesus forgave him, and then his body began to mend. Things move from the inside out, from a sense of forgiveness to physical healing.

Blessing Puny Little Resources

*O*ur minds tend to focus on the outside need. I go back again and again to the story of the feeding of the 5,000, because often in my life, I see incredible need, when the resources are ridiculously, and I mean ridiculously, low. Every time I look at the story, I find something new. Right now I am interested in the way Jesus helps change the people's mind-set. The disciples and the others look at the outside situation, make financial computations, and say the circumstances are impossible. I am struck by the fact that in Mark 6:39–40, Jesus tells everyone simply to sit down. One of the most important things we can often do in order to orient ourselves to the real issues is to stop. When someone is extremely anxious or extremely furious in our mission, I tend to suggest that they stop focusing on the issue, and take a walk along the river or in a park. Something happens when we take a breath. Mountains become mole hills again. Demonic enemies become simply troubled human beings again. Financial impossibilities become just long-term work. Sometimes there really are crises that need instantaneous actions, but so many things do not need that.

After Jesus tells the people to sit down, surprisingly, He gets things organized. Some wonder-workers make it sound as though organization is the antithesis of what they are doing. Yet Jesus in these same verses doesn't shy away from the need to get organized. He has the people sit down in groups of 50 or 100. Once we break up a project into smaller sections, something happens to us. We can eat an elephant after all, piece by piece. Breaking things down into smaller chunks does a lot of things for a person on the inside. The needs are all still the same, but something has happened to change one's perspective.

My co-worker, who helps feed thousands of people a year, sometimes reminds me of his view of the story. He doesn't deny the miraculous nature of what God did, but he says with a knowing look, "You know that out of 5,000-plus people, some of those people besides that little boy brought some food." Maybe they felt overwhelmed by the need. Maybe they felt that if they exposed their food in front of such a great number of people, it would all be gone immediately. Their sharing would turn out to be a hopeless task. But once those with food were sitting down with a smaller group of people, maybe 50 or 100, maybe they felt a little freer to share with those in their row. We don't know. But we do know that breaking overwhelming tasks into smaller chunks starts to change our insides.

Most importantly, Jesus speaks well of the little resources they had. Remembering this moment in the story overhauls the way I approach needs. With thousands of mouths to feed, I would be focusing on the outward circumstances and at the same time becoming inwardly resentful that the world had not dealt me a better hand. Five pieces of bread and two lit-tle fish for this group—what a horrible situation. Desperate prayers create a kind of inner gridlock and I can hardly think what to do next.

Yet Mark says Jesus blesses these puny little resources (6:41). To bless something means literally "to speak well" of it. For me, this approach, this internal attitude, is like an invest-ment in the abundance that God wants to give. I don't know how many times I have taken an envelope with perhaps a small gift and put my hands on it and prayed and spoke well of it. It's because I am learning that my inside approach will eventually work to the outside.

Tragic Things Happen to Tragic People

People who turn devotion upside down and focus on service sometimes tend to focus on outward circumstances. It is the clothing, or the rent money, or the food in hand, or the blanket in the winter, or the sheetrock after a storm—these are the important things. Well, they *are* important things. But it is the inside that counts the most. Recently we were closing out a phase of helping people after the hurricane that hit New York City. We had a case management component to the program, where we got involved with people's lives and helped in a small way to replace something that was lost in the hurricane—a mattress, a computer, some flooring. A few months ago we had a banquet for the people who had been hit hard by the hurricane. We celebrated that we survived. People gave testimonies. Some had big buildings and were in major bureaucratic discussions with insurance, FEMA, the city. But what people appreciated from our program was not the size of the gifts, which were relatively small, but the way they were treated. Graffiti workers brought cookies. They followed up the next day. They made the paperwork of the gift feel easy. They made the petitioners feel as though they were human beings. Because we focused on the inside of the person, people were much more appreciative than they were of entities who gave them much more major help.

I was with a person who had worked in the emergency rooms in New York City hospitals for most of her adult life. What a life! What is an emergency to me is just a normal day for her. "This is what I have learned," she said. "Tragic things happen to tragic people." At first I didn't understand what she meant. She didn't explain herself on that one, she left me to mull it over.

In one sense, I completely disagree with her. All one has to do is read a book like Job to see that there are all kinds of things going on in this cosmos that we will never understand and we have to be careful not to speak like Job's friends with their pat answers and their formulaic view of the world. In another sense, I think I know what she means. Hurting people hurt people. Then they get themselves in trouble. Some people see the world and everyone in it as their enemies, and they almost attract hardship and injury. Each event becomes a validation of their view and becomes a self-fulfilling prophecy for the next hurt. I remember reading about a worker who worked with teenagers in New York City. These teenagers became runaways and often in the end became prostitutes. "When I look at them," he said, "I see murdered children." These are children who have been hurt so badly in their early life that they act out their hurt, sabotaging themselves as they move through life. Like it or not, these people often spend more time in the emergency room than the rest of us.

When we are serious about learning to do good as a part of worship, as Isaiah instructs us, we find that part of our job is to walk alongside people and help them retell their story. It starts on the inside. Every person needs to have their story heard, but in the long-term, sometimes people also need to learn how to bury their failures and not frame them. The Word of God is great in this respect, because it continually reminds us that though we fail, we are not failures, but new creations.

Sadly enough, some hurts are not faced or healed, and then they become even more toxic. These hurts work together to become an ongoing script of self-pity. One of the most obvious examples to me in Jesus' life was the time at the Bethesda pool when Jesus saw a man who clearly had been there a long time (John 5:1–9). This time, Jesus doesn't spend many minutes listening to His list of sorrows. He simply asks, almost abruptly, it seems to me, "Do you want to be healed?" Like many of us, the man seemed absorbed in his inability to get into the pool and take advantage of the logistics of healing that he thinks will happen there. Since he has been an invalid for so long, clearly he has made this inability to get into the pool his story. Ironically, at first, he seems totally unaware that the Source of healing is standing next to him. Sorry, but I can't help but hear a hint of a whine from this man. What do you think? "Sir, I have no one to put me into the pool when the water is stirred up, and while I am going another steps down before me," he wheedles.

Jesus doesn't explain anything about healing, but simply gives him three clear instructions, starting with "Get up." Then He tells him to pick up his bed (carry your own load), and walk (literally "keep on walking"). Somehow, in some inner sea change, in some geologic shift inside the man, a benevolent tsunami of good comes into him. The universe changes within this man, as well as outside.

A Beautiful Woman in a Wheelchair

*P*art of upside-down devotion is deciding how we are going to see the things that happen to us. This week we had one of those unexpected moments in a Bible study. It was as though we were struck by lightning. We had a woman visiting our group from New Orleans. She was in a wheelchair. Her beautiful face glowed. In the group, she began to tell a bit of the story, and the group got more and more quiet. Her father was shot when she was two years old. During Hurricane Katrina, she had a tough journey of wading through water in her own neighborhood. Then she had some really rough experiences in the Astrodome before she finally got all the way to California. Eventually she returned to New Orleans. When she was 17 years old, a disgruntled friend who wanted her to talk to him came up and shot her at point blank range three times. She was partially paralyzed. She told how she cried out to God and asked why this happened when she was so young. She talked about being so confused and then walking into a Baptist church. She said somehow she immediately felt as though she had come home. One of the people there told her how to get "saved," in other words, rescued. She knew she needed it and she followed the woman's instructions.

"I never thought I would be here in New York sharing what has happened," she beamed. We eventually closed the Bible study time in prayer. No one left. Everyone continued to sit in their seats. Slowly and quietly, one by one, people shared their own difficulties and pressures and how they were dealing with them. A quiet, gentle Presence seemed to rule in the room. Some people cried. Finally people gathered around the young person in the wheelchair and hugged her. Many of them asked her to sign the card she had given them.

As a pastor, I have kept thinking about her story. The *why* questions come naturally to all of us. Why did this happen to her when she was so young? Why did she go to school that day when she was shot? Why did her young friend do this to her? Why wasn't she healed quickly? On and on the questions go. But somewhere and somehow she moved beyond those questions. She refused to allow that horrible, meaningless trauma become her script for life and decided to let it be used for good. The people in that room where she shared, including myself, will never be the same. This kind of devotion is an inside job.

In the book *The Heavenly Man*, the main character, Brother Yun, finds himself in prison many different times for his faith. Yet to me, reading about him, he seems like one of the freest people I have ever read about. How could that be? At one time, he helps a violent prisoner come to the Lord. Finally that prisoner is executed. Brother Yun and the other leaders were thereafter led out in a truck in the rain in order to shame them in front of the entire city. However, Brother Yun exulted in God because he was given the privilege to suffer for Him. The kinds of things this man went through are the kinds of things I see crippling people on the inside and making them bitter all the time. These hurts get framed, hung up in the gallery of their minds, and the pictures of pain never come down. The hurts cripple the person twice, once from the outside circumstances that happened, and a second time by becoming the poison that keeps the person from ever moving ahead. However, what God did on the inside of Brother Yun kept him free when all the circumstances on the outside would have stopped him.

At one point in my life, I was looking for a change, and I took a number of survival courses. These were courses where I would go out in the woods for a week (a far cry from my Manhattan job) and learn skills in case I didn't have food or matches or water or tools. One of the teachers, the best teacher there, said this one day: "There are two things you need when you are in a survival situation, skills and attitude. You need to learn the skills to survive. You also need an attitude that refuses to give up. Both things are very important. But if I had to choose one thing for survival, it would be attitude."

The night after my teacher said this, it was very cold. Icy rain was coming down, and I was sleeping alone in a cheap old tent. I woke up in the middle of the night and there was a puddle of icy water inside the tent. Part of my cheap sleeping bag was already wet. It seemed to be getting colder and colder. I began to shiver, and didn't feel as though I could do anything. I began to visualize what the others would say in the morning when they found me, cold and stiff, my life snuffed out by hypothermia. I was feeling more and more sorry for myself, with my cheap tent and shoddy sleeping bag. All the other campers had high-class equipment. It wasn't fair. Every minute felt like an hour. If only dawn would come. I became more and more gloomy as I shivered in the wet rain and listened to the wind. I didn't know what to do.

Then I thought of what my teacher said. I didn't have the skills, but I could have the attitude. When I started thinking that way, I realized I had all sorts of resources inside my tent. I started thinking about how a squirrel makes a nest by stuffing lots of leaves around its home. I found a plastic bag and protected my feet from the freezing wet sleeping bag. I put on all the clothes I could and stuffed the plastic bag and the dry part of the sleeping bag with every other thing I had that might provide even a bit of insulation. Once I got back into the sleeping bag, I was surprisingly warm, like a squirrel in its nest. I woke up to sunlight and warmth the next day, and I felt fine. Without the right attitude, I could have had a long, miserable, if not fatal, night. It's the inside job that counts when we think about almost anything, including service.

Drinks on the House

When we think about the inside stuff rather than the outside stuff, one more area of need always raises its head. People who get caught up with the passion of serving, of upside-down devotion to God, fall into this same trap and mind-set so often that the predicament has become a cliché. Sometimes these servants focus so much on the needs outside their families that they forget the needs inside their family. They are announcing drinks on the house while their own children are starving for milk.

In the early years here, I can remember some of the most difficult choices I would make. Sometimes, after a long, long day, I would be leaving for home to make it in time for the dinner that my wife had worked on and arranged for me and our little children. As I left the office worn out and frazzled, I would encounter one more person standing at the door, asking for help — food or clothing or some other emergency — often an emergency that would take some significant time. It was a tough choice for me. Do I do this one more thing for others, or do I respect my commitment and promise to my spouse and two little children? Sometimes I would say yes to the person standing at the door, and sometimes I would say no, and leave the person standing there on the street. It was always a tough choice for me. But now

I am glad I did not always say yes to the person on the street, which would have been a no to my own kids. In one sense, spending time on the "inside" with the family is the most significant thing we do on earth, assisting in those most primary relationships, helping those little ones be either capable or incapable of keeping their promises. When thinking about service, in an upside-down way, spending time with our own family on the "inside" helps them and us be capable of reaching out to the outside. We ignore this truth and pay a tough price.

principle #6
We Do One Thing,
Not a Hundred Things

"When my heart is overwhelmed: lead me to the rock that is higher than I" (PSALM 61:2 KJV).

"He who wants to do everything will never do anything."

—ANDRÉ MAUROIS

The Right Not to Feel Overwhelmed

The subway sign had a picture of a woman sitting and trying to hold more packages than she could handle. Three had already fallen to the floor. Two toddlers were holding on to her rumpled coat, and they were crying. The woman's tired face looked desperate. The subtitle simply said, "Overwhelmed—overcome completely in mind or feelings by superior force or numbers."

We understand. People who have a heart to serve often feel overwhelmed. These are servants who have a compassionate heart and see the importance of not making worship to God be some kind of lip service. They know the hypocrisy of the religious people who pass by the suffering man on the road to Jericho and find an excuse not to do anything. They see the piles of needs all around them and work hard not to turn away anyone. People in need see quickly that this is a person who says yes to providing help, and they are drawn to that person like moths to a light. But sometimes it feels as though they are drawn like vultures to a carcass.

We understand. Soon these servants feel overwhelmed, and eventually experience extreme burnout along with exhaustion and resentment. They serve others for a year or two and then retreat from the places of greatest need because they respond to every need. How sad that these people who have the tenderest hearts to help others cannot stay in the places where they might help the most.

Deep down, we all know that we have an unexpressed right not to live a life feeling constantly overwhelmed. Yet many who know that devotion is more than songs and liturgy find themselves in a place where they are trying to hold up too many packages, and several people are pulling on to their rumpled coat at the same time, and they are all crying.

We feel like the one sane batter at a batting machine that has gone crazy. The pitches keep coming faster and faster, and we frantically take a swing at as many pitches as we can. We find ourselves in an old-time *I Love Lucy* show, where the conveyer belt of goods is going faster and faster and we are doing a poorer and poorer job of packing them. Before you know it, we are a purveyor not of kindness, but of resentment, feeling more and more stress and anger and not completely knowing why.

I have watched a few people, some of them struggling with mental illness, intentionally rewrite their script when they were flooded with needs. It started with a decision. They told themselves, "I refuse to be overwhelmed." They stopped reciting the old script, "I am so overwhelmed I don't know what to do." They started repeating their new script. "I will get through this." Then regardless of the number of things coming at them, they took charge of one thing at a time. I was amazed at the results as they stayed consistent.

How wise Paul of Tarsus was when he felt as though he was against the ropes. In the middle of a storm of problems, he makes this comment about one of the challenges: "We are not ignorant of [Satan's] designs" (2 Corinthians 2:11). Whether the problem is unforgiveness or stress, we need to be aware of what is at work. Being overcome by superior numbers is not a new problem. David understood about forces larger than us bearing down on us. He said, "When my heart is overwhelmed: lead me to the rock that is higher than I" (Psalm 61:2 KJV).

Where is that higher rock? The overwhelmed person often has to do fewer things. A song from an old film on Francis of Assisi caught the flavor of this approach.

If you want your dream to be
Take your time, go slowly
Do few things but do them well
Heartfelt work grows purely.
"THE LITTLE CHURCH" BY DONOVAN

Every person who turns devotion right side up and makes service a primary part of life has to confront the issue of how much to do. When we try to do everything, we destroy the things we can do. This is one of the great joys of life—finding the things we are to do so that we can pour our heart into those few things. It means refusing to do the things we aren't to do.

The Midwife and the Executioner

ecently the needs of the city were overwhelming me. I got away for a night or so in Long Island. I got up early and walked a long way to a lonely rocky beach that looked out at the ocean. The sun was beginning to rise. I let my eyes rest on the ocean that seemed to go on and on forever. It was so vast, and I thought about all the teaming life that I could not surmise going on underneath the surface of the reflection of light that I saw at the top of the ocean. I thought of the fisherman's prayer, "Your sea is so wide and my boat is so small." Then I thought of all the people in New York City—they were like a sea. The vastness, the complexity of their swarming needs seemed like an ocean, so overwhelming. When we think of all the things we could do to serve God, we can think of a hundred projects in a minute. There is so much good that could be done. Yet for a servant in an area of need, it is much wiser to think thus—do one thing, not a hundred things.

A gardener at a botanic garden put it well. She was bemoaning the fact that she would have to pull up some beautiful flowers in order for another group of flowers to thrive. But she has to pull up flowers all the time. She simply said, "Every gardener is both a midwife and an executioner." In order for us to be the midwife of some dreams in our lives, we will have to be the executioner of many others. When someone comes to me with a dream to serve others in some special way, I am also listening to hear how many other dreams they have. Is this one of a menu of wonderful possibilities, or is this that particular dream of service, the one they have chosen regardless of circumstances?

So how do we know what to do? If there is no God, then we are pretty much on our own. We have to make the choices, and be the executioner using our own devices. It doesn't really work that well. In his letter to the Romans, Paul indicates that we have a choice, but really it is a choice of who will lead us. He also says that all who are led by the Spirit of God are the children of God (Romans 8:14). If we are led only by what we think is right, or respond to all the things that are good in terms of service, we will take on layers and layers of responsibility and eventually we will collapse, like a roof that has quietly taken on more and more snow until it finally falls in. How can that be? Each snowflake seemed so light. Surely we can take on just a few more snowflakes.

Isaiah tells the story of the people of God as they work energetically for a plan. We have mentioned Isaiah's approach before. The people of God are willing to work very hard for this plan; it just doesn't happen to be God's plan. He calls them stubborn children "who carry out a plan, but not mine, and who make an alliance, but not of my Spirit" (Isaiah 30:1). Isaiah uses the same phrase that Paul uses—it is not a plan of God's Spirit. Isaiah paints a picture of these poor pathetic people, working faster and faster, finding faster and faster vehicles to move about in, but instead of saving them, it will only make their destruction come faster (v. 16). A little later, he describes how God's guidance works. This description may give us insight on God's guidance, and help us know what to do and what not to do. "And your ears shall hear a word behind you, saying, 'This is the way, walk in it,' when you turn to the right or when you turn to the left" (v. 21). As we have said before, the inside work makes the outside work happen.

Those who are service-oriented don't want to spend time sitting around, they want to get out there and do something. But in the Book of James there is a promise that we will receive wisdom if we ask for it (James 1:5). We are also told that wisdom is the beginning, the principal thing for everything else (Proverbs 4:7). In the middle of some of Jesus' most intense activity, He withdrew into the desolate places and prayed. The choice of Greek words seems to indicate that He would do this often (Luke 5:16).

When Jesus Says No

*O*ne of the best ways to hear God's voice is to take a day off once a week. It is really critical, and people who are "devoted" forget it all the time. They think they have to be doing something constantly in order to be pleasing to God. No, it is doing something at the right time. Taking a day off is one of the "big ten"—it's right there in the Ten Commandments. If we don't take a day of rest, in the end sickness becomes our rest. A day of rest gives us a chance to see God's invisible love through the visible circumstances. It is stepping out of the picture for a bit to hear what God has for us to do next. It's like a time-out, where the quarterback gets to take a bit of time to walk over and talk to the coach face-to-face.

The Bible says we are to be the head and not the tail (Deuteronomy 28:13). When we plan a Sabbath, someone always has something extremely urgent we must do on that day. All we have to say is, "Thank you, but I have a previous commitment." Your previous commitment may be to lie in bed and drink coffee, but few people will ever ask you what your previous commitment is. Incidentally, the Sabbath is a great time for community service workers to spend time with their peers. You may be dealing with people in deep need all week, whether they are adults or youth or children. But these people should not have to carry the burden of filling your personal needs for friendship. You should spend time with your peers on your Sabbath, not secretly make it another workday by scheduling time with those who depend on you in other ways.

Of course, we can take a Sabbath time every day too. One of the greatest revelations of my life was that if I didn't plan my day, someone else would do it for me. It is amazing how many service-oriented Christians skip this need for extended daily time with God. No wonder we try to do everything. Yet we have to plan it and structure our day around it. Our mission doesn't answer the phone until 10:00 A.M. so that people can have more time for prayer in the morning. After so many years, nobody complains that we don't answer the phone at 9:00 A.M. It is so important to make the decision for quiet time.

Of course, in the New Testament, Martha becomes the poster child for the distracted, stressed-out, irritable worker, doing many good and necessary things, but somehow missing the point. Mary just sits there listening to Jesus, while Martha has to do all the hosting work, and she finally has enough. Martha is also the one that many service-oriented people think got a bad rap. I mean, someone needed to make the dinner. But Mary does the "one thing necessary," and that one thing is listening to Jesus. The other things can be done at another time. Most of us have stopped to listen to the demands of so many voices that we really don't know what to do next; we have forgotten the *one thing* necessary (Luke 10:38–42). Instead we try to do a hundred things.

This one thing necessary doesn't always mean sitting. In the chapter preceding the story about Mary and Martha, Jesus "sets his face to go to Jerusalem" (Luke 9:51). There were a lot of places Jesus could have gone to, and a lot of these places would have been easier places for Jesus. By going to Jerusalem, he rejected all the other places he could have gone. That is the way life is—whatever we select involves rejecting a ton of other options. He knew what he had to move toward.

Paul understood how important it was to be led by the Spirit. He was clearly brilliant. He could have stayed pastoring a megachurch in Jerusalem. Clearly he understood the strategic importance of Jerusalem. On the other hand, with his smarts, he probably could have established a tent-making business empire, blessing people all over the Mediterranean with shelter and making a lot of money to further the gospel too. But Paul knew that the Holy Spirit was leading him to be a minister to the Gentiles (Romans 15:16). That was his calling and this calling determined what he was to do, and what he was not to do.

We need the same instructions, or else as servants we get overwhelmed and try to hold up too many packages. How do we know what we are to do? Do the one thing that Mary did in Luke 10, and then you will know what to do and when, without trying to do it all. The desire to hear God's voice is the beginning. We learn to pray by praying. We learn to listen by listening. We learn to obey by obeying. Then we learn to do by doing.

In a sense, saying no to things is a part of God's heart. We are told in the Bible that "God is love" (1 John 4:16), and isn't the essence of love saying no to a lot of other things? Parents sometimes say no to a particular career choice in order to spend more time with their children. A woman says no to all the other men she could have dated in order to marry the one man. A man says no to an outing he loves in order to spend time with his son. Whenever we love anyone or anything, we are focusing our attention and forgetting all the other things we could be doing. Jesus said a lot of noes to a lot of things. Just think—He could have been doing so many other things on that day He was killed like a criminal.

principle #7
There's a Time to Be Angry, Not Tolerant

"Note then the kindness and the severity of God"
(ROMANS 11:22, PAUL).

"Few are guilty, but all are responsible."

—ABRAHAM JOSHUA HESCHEL, *THE PROPHETS*

The Man Who Refused to Work

*A*ccording to Scripture, anger gives the devil an access code to our heart. "Give no opportunity to the devil" (Ephesians 4:27). So much of life is covered in the first few pages of the Bible. Clearly, in the early story, Cain is "very angry" because his brother's offering is accepted by God. Like a loving counselor, God comes to Cain and asks about his anger. God warns Cain that Cain is about to be victimized by his own anger. Sin is just off the radar screen and ready to pounce. "Sin is crouching at the door. Its desire is for you, but you must rule over it" (Genesis 4:7). Cain doesn't listen, and he ends up murdering his own brother.

In an earlier book in this series, I wrote about anger becoming a cage. Some of the people in our mission have earlier gone to prison because their anger/fear pounced upon them and took control over them. Jesus' brother warns us that "the anger of man does not produce the righteousness of God" (James 1:20). Most of us know the sensation of anger taking hold on us so that problems and hurts grow all out of proportion to what is good for us or others. Anger can grip us and shake us like a dog shakes a rabbit.

Yet there may be a time for anger. Joe was a person who came to our mission for food and to be with us for some kind of strange fellowship he alone had in mind He seemed to thrive on irritating people. In the hustle-bustle of a Wednesday night meal, he would make a point of annoying the person next to him and demanding extra condiments incessantly from the one serving him. Most of the other people in the group would help clean up or assist our meal in some other way. Joe refused to do so. He would stay for Bible study but he would use the time to divert the group from the point and make contentious comments to the leaders. He lived on the street, and many on the street didn't like him for this behavior either.

People at Graffiti don't give up, and they were tolerant of him for years. Joe took advantage of their tolerance. In fact, he seemed to thrive on taking advantage of these people.

One day we heard some sad news. A precious young man named Victor had died. He had been a part of our group and even gone to stay at our rehab program in the country for a while. Victor was a bit slow-thinking, but very kind to everyone and he was always willing to help others. Apparently Victor felt sick as he was traveling and took aspirin again and again in an effort to make himself feel better. The amount that he took eventually killed him.

Our mission was crushed at the news and we held a memorial service so that people from the street could gather and remember this gentle individual. Everyone was welcome, and these services were always a special time where people could remember the good things about someone who had passed away. Joe came to the gathering. His comments about Victor during the service were obnoxious and insulting. The room was filled with an embarrassed pause after he spoke. In a way, he ruined this special time for everyone else.

Afterward when we were alone, I told Joe how angry I was. I told him that he could eat a meal but that he had to take a breather from the Bible study group. After a few weeks, he could do something to be accepted back into the Bible study. It wasn't a hard thing. He would have to do one thing to help the mission, maybe stack up the chairs after the meal or clean the tables. He had never done anything before.

I think it would have been wrong to simply be tolerant of Joe at that time. He was part of our community, and he needed to hear how angry I was. I couldn't pretend, and I think he needed to have some consequence or requirement. Some accountability was a part of God's grace. In this circumstance, a mild toleration would have been worse than anger. For better or for worse, Joe was a part of our community, our tribe, so to speak, and he needed some in-house confrontation.

Incidentally, Joe refused to do even the smallest thing to help at the mission, even though he continued to receive food at our mealtime. Every week I reminded him that all he had to do to be accepted again into our Bible study was to do one thing to help us as we fed others. Week after week he refused. I noticed that our Bible study time went so much better without him. Some people began to accept the Lord in the group. I never realized how much Joe had sabotaged our group until he was gone. He never did come back to our group, even though he was repeatedly invited to do one task for the mission in order to come back. Before he died, I had a chance to visit him in a hospital. When I came in, he was on the phone talking to his sister. He was just as obnoxious and demanding and insulting to her.

A Runaway and a Car Thief

*I*n a strange way, a certain kind of anger means you are family. I have thought repeatedly about a deeply troubled 14-year-old boy I encountered when I first arrived in New York City. One day he ran away, and we spent the night looking for him in the abandoned buildings and haunts of our neighborhood at the time. For me, going through these dark buildings at night was like a scene from a Halloween horror movie. Eventually the runaway returned. I was talking to him in front of the storefront when his brother, who was two years older than he, approached. The brother grabbed him by the front of his shirt and flung him against the wall. After a river of curses, the older brother said, "How stupid can you be? Don't you ever do that again!" After a few more choice words, he released him and let him drop to the ground. Then he stomped off.

This is the first thing that younger brother said after the incident. "Gee, I never knew my brother loved me." What seemed destructive anger from my context felt like love from his context. Sometimes anger is like that—it lets you know that you are inside the circle, not outside the circle. Of course, this does not condone anger accompanied by abuse. Acquaintances, however, only get polite niceties. Family members get something else. We know this truth in our guts. It was the Pharisees whom Jesus seemed to be most angry at. Yet they were in many ways the ones who shared the most with Jesus. They honored the Word of God and believed in the Resurrection.

If we don't have a context, sometimes it is hard to understand when anger is appropriate and when it is not. I remember one time some people thought I wasn't being Christian when I chewed a homeless man out before he came in to have a meal with us. What they didn't see was he had a metal strip and was just trying to break into someone's car outside our mission. I'd known him for a long time. He needed someone to tell him to stop it. He knew better than that. I told him to stop breaking into cars; but if he was going to break into cars anyway, at least have the decency not to do it around the church as we were offering our meal. He knew he was wrong. He muttered his agreement and he stopped his theft. Then he had a meal with the rest of us.

Here is the point for those who wish to turn devotion to God upside down and let service be at the heart of what we do: gentle tolerance can be cruel. It is cruel not to confront the person who is stealing. There is nothing Christian about that kind of tolerance. It is cruel to spoil a child—long term this approach only prepares the child to be a selfish adult.

Certain spheres of responsibility make anger appropriate. If I am at a restaurant, and the children at the next table are smearing peas on the wall and pouring lemonade on the seats, I will just gently smile and be amicably tolerant. They are not my children. But if *my* children are doing that, they will see an entirely different side of my personality. Many children know "the look" from their parents. "The look" from a parent says many things, but one thing it says is that although the child is in a public place now, like a restaurant or a church or a shopping mall, there will be consequences for the child now or later on. Usually, if the parent is consistent, "the look" is all he or she needs.

This kind of anger doesn't imply violent behavior. Whether it is in a nation or a parent or other relative, violence is almost always a sign of weakness. It says that I cannot influence the other person or group in any other way but force. It is a position of weakness and force is the only method it has. We are smarter than that. A position of strength has many ways to influence others. So, given the context, anger doesn't imply violence. In church, we are told to be angry but not to sin. We are not to let the sun set on our anger — we are to address it in a healthy way that day, starting with a one-on-one discussion.

Adults Who Act Like Children

*A*s people mature in ministry, I think that they intuitively see the place for severity. People who work with children know that children will expend a lot of energy to get attention. If they can't get attention by doing well, they will try to get it by acting out. And some learn that they can get a lot of things because others will just placate them. Some adults have developed those same temper tantrum skills to survive on the street. A refusal to reward that kind of behavior may look like severity, but it helps the adult know that there are other more successful ways to cope.

Sometimes a meal for adults who have a variety of issues may feel like a scene from the fourth grade. Sometimes I find myself walking into a shouting match in progress. I usually choose the saner-acting person or group. If I don't know them, I tell them my first name. Then I ask them their name. Then, addressing them by their name, I respectfully ask them to come outside with me so that we can talk quietly. As with children, the attention fuels the fight. Removing a person from the environment is a start. It also takes the wind out of the sails of both parties. I usually refuse to talk to the noisier party until he or she calms down.

Sometimes in community ministry we are dispensing goods. In such a case, mercy can be crueler than justice. It is unkind to feel sorry for the third person in line who pleads for sandwiches for his friends when there are 200 people who have been waiting in line. If an exception is made, then experience has taught me that every single person afterward asks for an exception. The people who have been dutifully waiting will never get a sandwich. It sounds harsh to say no, but strictness is the kindest thing to do. When these kinds of difficulties arise, we have learned that co-workers may not understand. We always tell workers to wait to work out disagreements in private. We learned this working with children, but it works in all the ministries, and it is right from the Bible (Matthew 18).

In the Bible, two truths are often put side by side. Martin Luther, the reformer, often called these truths paradoxes. On the one hand, God is merciful, gracious, kind, generous, tolerant, gentle. On the other hand, it is an idiotic thing to take God for a fool. That is what we do when we act like hypocrites. We act as though we are God-honoring on the outside, impressing others, stupidly forgetting that God, the One we are pretending to honor, isn't taken in by any of these petty charades. He sees our heart, our motives, our mind. God can be severe.

Paul of Tarsus has taught us a lot about grace and mercy, that there are no works of righteousness that we can do to earn our way to God. If we ever imply that there is some religious act we can do to earn God's acceptance, Paul gets livid, as he does in the letter to the Galatians. It is only according to His mercy that God saves us. Yet in talking about our acceptance with God, Paul doesn't only talk about grace.

> *Note then the kindness and the severity of God: severity toward those who have fallen, but God's kindness to you, provided you continue in his kindness. Otherwise you too will be cut off.*
>
> (ROMANS 11:22).

Paul says that? It is easy for me to visualize a god who is only mercy, and it is easy for me to visualize a god who is only severity. But only Christianity presents the God who through the Cross shows His mercy for us and also takes on the severe consequences of our actions (Romans 3:26). This God is not someone to trifle with.

Some people know how to express anger appropriately. Maybe they have simply an intuitive sense, or a certain kind of personality, or positive role models growing up. Others of us have to learn. We all know the parents who speak to the child in a sickly sweet voice even though it is clear they are really furious. This parent thinks that it is a virtue to be benevolent even when the child is misbehaving. It probably just confuses the child with that sweet voice and that hidden fury. The parent endures and endures and endures and then what finally happens? The parent explodes and responds to some action of the child in a wildly inappropriate way. Other parents are angry and shout all the time, but never take disciplinary action. They don't know that you've got to save your fire for the big battles, not every little petty conflict. The child eventually just ignores their anger.

The one who decides to turn devotion right side up in service will have to deal with anger, both wrong anger and right anger. Some people who are called to serve just patiently endure all kinds of abusive behavior from others and never say a word. Eventually they say that they just quit and can't take it. Others shout and are grouchy all the time. No one in the end takes them seriously. Every little incident is World War III.

The Art of Showing Anger

Every group will find its own way to deal with anger. At Graffiti we have learned from experience that there is a price paid when we receive someone else's anger on the street. Our head knows that the anger is ridiculous and not really aimed at us, but our heart still takes it in. The shouting and abuse still hurts. We find that it is important for co-workers to have some time to share their frustrations in a redeeming way, to vent concerning how difficult a particular situation or person is. This kind of shared frustration becomes smaller, because everyone in the room understands what the person is feeling. In the end, we may be able to laugh at ourselves or the ridiculousness of the whole situation. A little self-deprecating humor never hurts either.

Showing anger in serving is an art, an art that requires both timing and context. Even dogs know that sometimes the leader of the pack may need to growl to set some boundaries, but the leader doesn't have to bite. Within his own tribe, the warrior may need to flash his sword, but he doesn't have to use it. Good coaches know this. The best teachers I had in school were not the cream puffs. The best teachers were both kind and severe, and gave consequences for student work that was less than our best, as well as attention when we did well.

Even anger can be used in the service of others. There is an art to knowing the times that you need to show your anger and when not to. "Good sense makes one slow to anger, and it is his glory to overlook an offense" (Proverbs 19:11). Most offenses don't warrant anger. I learned a lot from an older airplane pilot many years ago. We were working together each week to start a shelter for others. The work required long meetings and lots of juggling to get things started. This man was invariably gentle and good humored, and earned the respect of the group with his good sense. We worked together for more than a year, and I only saw him get angry one time. It was late in a meandering meeting, where one person was incessant in his self-pity and wandering observations, just when we needed to focus in order to open the shelter. Finally, like a lightning flash, the pilot's eyes glared and he said one sentence with severity. It was a thunderclap on the group. He told the whining member to be quiet and straighten up. The person did so, and then the group, after a stunned pause of deadly silence, got back on track to start the shelter, which we did successfully.

Because of that pilot's personality, that one sentence at the right time was enough. In the context of that group which had become a family of sorts, the one sentence was all that was needed. He showed me that anger can be used to great effect when used appropriately. Most of us, however, shoot off our guns at the wrong things with the wrong motives, and it doesn't really work the righteousness of God.

When we serve God with people who are in great need, we will sometimes need to act as a shepherd. We will have the obligation to provide a safe place for healing in the group. To be honest, sometimes people will attempt to sabotage that safe place in a variety of ways. The saboteur may realize what he or she is doing, or he or she may be completely unaware. In either case, we will find that sometimes we will need to be both kind and severe. A casual observer might not understand. Sometimes being tolerant to the one who is taking advantage of others won't work.

Abraham Joshua Heschel, the Hebrew teacher we mentioned earlier, did a lot of reflecting on the anger of God. He knew that as we looked at life, there were times that it would be wrong not to be indignant. He had lost family members in the Holocaust and reflected on the trajectory of his own society toward that destruction. Heschel believed God clearly saw some of the things we do as calamities. Clearly some of the things in our society are extremely unjust. Heschel said that anger in God is the personal dimension of justice. Some oppression is so horrendous, it is inappropriate not to be angry.

Usually in the Bible, the anger of God ends with an invitation. God will not be angry forever. It is God's steadfast love that lasts forever. We see the same thing in Jesus. When He talks to those who are closest to Him in beliefs, the Pharisees who claim to honor God's Word, we can almost sense the exclamation points in His sentences. "'Woe to you, scribes and Pharisees, hypocrites! . . . You also outwardly appear righteous to others, but within you are full of hypocrisy and lawlessness'" (Matthew 23:25, 28). The whole section is so severe toward those who act like hypocrites. But even at His most severe, Jesus almost always extends an invitation. At the end of His lengthy challenge, and He doesn't seem to hide His anger because He cares so much, He laments. He looks at the city and He says, "How often would I have gathered your children together as a hen gathers her brood under her wings, and you were not willing!" (Matthew 23:37). Let's be like Jesus, and when there is a time to be angry, not tolerant, let's end with an invitation to be enfolded in the wings of a motherly care.

principle #8
We Give Services, Not Money

"Let love be genuine" (ROMANS 12:9, PAUL).

*"You cannot help men permanently by doing
for them what they could and should do for themselves."*

—WILLIAM JOHN HENRY BOETCKER

"Please Help Me"

*H*e sounded as though he had said the same thing a thousand times. His face was weary and his clothes were dirty as he stood in front of the grocery store. "Please help me," he said. "I just got out of the hospital and I just need money to get back to my family in Virginia." I don't remember the rest of what he said. Everything in me was telling me he had other problems. I told him I couldn't give him any money, but I went into the store to buy him something to eat.

By the time I returned, he was talking to another man. I could tell by the man's posture that he was indecisive about what to do but wanted to do something. Eventually the man, with some hesitation, reached into his pocket and pulled out a few bills and gave them to the man. As soon as the man got the bills, he started heading around the building. Since I had bought him some food, I followed him to give it to him, whether he wanted the food or not. By this time, the man who had pleaded for money had a cell phone to his ear, and he was moving fast. I wanted to follow him. Was he heading toward a liquor store in the area? What was really going on inside of him as he gave his lines, over and over? I finally caught up with him, but he did not want to talk. He took the food hardly breaking his stride, with the phone to his ear, and he kept moving.

I continued to think about the body language of the man who gave him money. I suppose everyone has been in his shoes. He wanted to help, but didn't know exactly what to do. He suspected that the money might be going toward other things than what was requested, but what if the poor man's story were true and the giver said no? Perhaps the man who gave the money was a Christian, and he had another layer of words telling him to give when people ask. Deep down he knew he didn't have much time to spend with this man, and so in the end he reached in his pocket and gave him something, so that he could be on his way. Maybe he even wondered if what he did was right as he pushed his cart down the aisles of the grocery store.

There were times in our work in New York City when I felt as though I was asked a hundred times a day for money or food or help by people on the street. The cynical part of me feels as though I have heard every story — the needing gas story, the money for baby formula story, the death of the mother story, the job in New Jersey story, and on and on. I remember years ago working in San Francisco with an agency that helped people who were on the street. I worked with a Franciscan sister who, to my young eyes, seemed to have been working with people on the street forever. She told me that 90 percent of the requests were cons, and the percentage kept going up. At the time, I felt she had become hardened and couldn't really see all that was around her, but I don't feel that way anymore.

It doesn't really matter. Con people need help too. It just might not be the kind of help they think they need. I have no inkling what I would do if I were gripped by some of the circumstances and addictions that are normal for many of these people. So what do you do when people ask you for help? Different Christians come up with different answers, and I certainly don't think that there is only one way.

But here is a realization that has helped me with many things in church — you often learn more from people by doing a task together with them than by just talking to them. Sometimes for me, having a project, no matter how small, to do together is more helpful than a counseling session. To me, this truth is just in our nature. It is easy for me to give someone a dollar, but it is time, doing something together, that people really need.

A person who works a lot with government programs and youth recently commented to me that no one was ever affected by a program. They were always affected by a *person* in the program. We are always changed by relationships, not programs, not dictates, not money.

So what do we do if someone asks for money? Perhaps we could say, "I can't give you any money, but what if I buy you a bagel? Let's go together to the store and I will get you and myself a bagel." If the person agrees, then you are embarking on a little project, and more importantly, you are spending time together. We recommend that men make this offer to men, and women make this offer to women. The problem with this approach is that it takes more time. In a big city, you can't do this for everyone who asks. But as we said before, that is what love is all about. It is making the choice and saying that I reject doing one thing, so that I can select doing something with you.

Sowing and Reaping

heard someone say this on TV and it has changed my life: "Entering the kingdom of God is leaving the realm of buying and selling and entering the realm of sowing and reaping." We often think in terms of buying and selling like being at McDonald's. I give you this dollar and you give me a dollar hamburger. If I don't get it in a few minutes, I am going to get mad. That is the contract we have between each other. On the streets they sometimes call it the "favor bank"—I did something for you and now you need to do something for me. When we carry this approach into our relationships, we will almost always be disappointed. Marriage doesn't work that way. Neither does family nor friendship. We will just end up resentful.

Sowing and reaping is another matter. When I was a teenager, I went with my dad to work on some farms he had. He used to make this comment, but never explained it: "No farmer is an atheist." As a teenager, I used to think to myself, *Well of course there are farmers who are atheists—that is ridiculous.* But now that I am older, I think my father was saying something else.

First of all, no farmer really thinks he is in control of things. A hailstorm or rain at the wrong time can change everything, and there may not be much he can do about that. Perhaps a person going to work in Silicon Alley in New York can go to his cubicle in the city and create the illusion that he is in control, but a farmer knows better. Second of all, a farmer knows deep down that he or she doesn't really produce anything. Farmers may plant seeds and may cultivate and make conditions opportune for growth, but farmers can't manufacture a single harvest. Harvests just come in due season.

The fact that harvests come in due season points to the third thing that farmers know. Things take time. You plant and then you wait. It is not like buying a fast-food burger. Most things of value take time. Investing in people takes time. And with people, you are not sure when the harvest may come.

Farmers usually know the season when harvest will come. We often do not know. I have a friend who was given a blooming orchid. He put it in his office. Eventually the flower faded, but he kept tending it. He knew nothing about orchids. Six months passed and no more flowers came. A year passed and still no more flowers. Still, he kept watering the plant. Eighteen months later a flower bloomed again. He was so surprised. That is the way it is when we invest in people. We don't know when the results may come.

So now I don't get so resentful when things don't happen with people when I expect them to. I see myself as someone who is sowing seeds, like a farmer. Things take time. We are investing in children at Graffiti by offering children's programs. We are investing in youth and adults by having times when workers can work with them on training and values.

And when someone in deep need asks for help, we want to invest in them too. We don't want to just give them a dollar, even when that is what they think they want. We want to find something where we spend time together. In fact, everything becomes a matter of sowing and reaping—our marriage, our family, our particular ministry. Sometimes we don't know when the harvest will come. Sometimes it may occur beyond our lifetime. Abraham didn't see the full harvest that God promised him, but wow, did the harvest come! I see myself as one of Abraham's children, as do billions of people. It just took a few thousand years. Every harvest has its season.

I Cannot Help You Unless . . .

So our mission has made the commitment that we provide services, not money. By making this commitment, we remind ourselves that we are investing time in people as we set goals together, whether they are small goals, such as getting a bagel, or they are large goals, such as getting a job. We want to invest in people, not just give someone some change.

We know that when we give money, we are often participating in someone's addiction. Even though the person asking may feel desperate for the money, giving money in that way really does people an injustice. We sometimes tell a person, "I cannot help you anymore unless you let me get involved in your life." The person may get angry but that is OK. Love never promised that the other person would be appreciative. We have also learned that if we give out money, we are seen differently. Money is a low form of power, but it is a power. The recipient sees the church or the Christian as their banker and nothing else, when there is so much more to their healing.

I have read in the past about certain parts of the world where the church has publicized requests to individuals not to give to beggars so that the church and others can give more comprehensive and coordinated care. Bouncing from person to person begging for money is not really a long-term solution. The Bible says to "let love be genuine," in other words, let love not be hypocritical (Romans 12:9). This instruction means to me that sometimes we have to take a hard look at how we are showing love to a person who is evidently trapped by an addiction to alcohol or drugs or something else. Giving a dollar could be just a way to move on without having to think about the person much more.

Many years ago, the man who helped to start Graffiti was on a bus in Atlanta and sat next to a man who was going to a pro-life demonstration. They got into an animated discussion about the issues revolving around the pro-life movement. The man from Graffiti eventually issued a challenge — "Since you live in New Jersey, why don't you go to Graffiti to help the poor if you have compassion on those who are most vulnerable?"

The man took up the challenge and said, "OK, I think I will." He called me and started coming to a program where we offered free sandwiches. He started bringing soup every Saturday. He listened to people's stories. He was bold and offered to pray with them, even on the street. And he always came back the next week. Eventually he began teaching a group huddled in the storefront after getting sandwiches, and became an anointed Bible teacher. Miracles happened. People left their addictions and started new lives. People got healed, and praised God. He helped people get jobs, and even trained them in being an artist. He invested his life in these people. He didn't just give a little money and move on. He gave something much more; he gave himself. He had entered a world of sowing and reaping, and it was really a wondrous experience.

At the same time, we continue to learn that we are not the Savior, and we cannot function for long in the role of rescuer. Sometimes when we find ourselves doing all the work for someone, making appointments, resolving issues, we have to tell the other person, "I feel that I am working harder than you are." Then we have to stop because our actions are becoming unhealthy for the other person. If we accept the role of rescuer, we eventually become the persecutor, because we find the person is not doing all the things we think they should, and we blame them for it.

If we are thinking about genuine love, we need to think about what we are really doing when we give money. So much of our story is included in the first few pages of the Bible. Even before we rebelled, we were to work the garden and keep it (Genesis 2:15). As many have pointed out, to deprive humans of meaningful work is to deprive them of the proper balance God has for them. We were never designed simply to receive. Deep within us is the need to do something meaningful and helpful. We deceive ourselves and others when we think by providing everything for someone we are doing them justice.

Recently one of our new Graffiti sites has had to struggle with this sense of wholeness again. The site was started in one of the most challenging and depressed neighborhoods in the city. What good is it to be an advocate for someone who is being evicted and to procure funds for them, when the tenant will do the same thing again? Is that really fair to the landlord? What good is it to help a poor person receive a grant if it keeps the person in the same dependent pattern? These are hard questions that have to be asked when working in poorer communities. For me, this is where the church comes in. The church provides the group of believers, and then the group helps in transformation, in accountability, in helping someone to walk on their own. The group can also say the hard thing when needed. Otherwise we become another group of social workers, sometimes hurting more than helping.

The Power of a Group

With all the competing plans and theories to address the problems of our society and poverty, it was such a practical discovery to see how powerful the church is in action. When God works to transform a person's life, it is never done for the person alone. An alcoholic in the park can accept Jesus 20 times a day, and some of them do, playing Christians like a fiddle. Often, unless there is some group accountability, not much else will happen for the alcoholic. Groups are one of the most important ways that the Spirit of God flows. They provide love, support, and accountability for the person involved in great change. A group encourages a person not just to receive, but to give. If the person doesn't give as well as receive, the group will intuitively nudge the person in that direction. Alcoholics Anonymous utilized these energies in recent times, but the church has used them for thousands of years. The Greek word for *church* in the Greek New Testament is often translated as to literally mean "called out." But in usage in the first-century world, it often simply meant "group."

How powerful it was for me to see the church/group in action in our original storefront. It was challenging the new believers in Christ, laughing with them, pointing out the excuses they were using to stay in a bad place, training them to endure. But the church/group was not just giving out money.

By refusing to give money, we can go to the other extreme also. We can say that troubled people simply need to help themselves, and we can justify our position with examples. The danger of this position is that we can use it as an excuse to do very little, saying poor people have to help themselves or it will do no good. This extreme can tend to "ghettoize" entire communities in need. We leave them at the bottom rung of the ladder and use our philosophy to justify our inactivity. We can put a group of people in need or a territory in a kind of economic apartheid, saying that they must help themselves. This to me is like telling someone with broken legs that they just need to take a brisk walk around the block and they will be OK.

But we do want to be about helping people walk. We want to aid people to stand up and walk on their own as much as they can. Otherwise, something human is taken away from them. The answer, I think, for the upside-down servant, is not in giving some money. It is to be involved in healing. In the Book of Acts, Peter and John are walking up to the Temple to pray. Surely this is the way to devotion. But they encountered a man who was being carried by other people. He had been that way since birth. He was being carried so that he could ask for money from people as they went to pray. Peter and John didn't give him any money, however. Instead, they looked at him very directly and told him to look at them. Peter told the lame man that he had no money. Instead, Peter told the man to get up and walk. Then he took him by the right hand and raised him up. The power of healing was all around those actions, and the man walked (Acts 3:1–10). That is what we want to be about—not just giving a man a dollar on our way to worshipping God, but to be helping people to walk, to walk on their own. Then they will not need someone to carry them so that they can just beg for little dollars. Helping someone to walk is turning our worship times upside down.

principle #9
We Offer Choices, Not Goodies

"I have set before you life and death, blessing and curse. Therefore choose life" (DEUTERONOMY 30:19).

"Did you ever have to finally decide? And say yes to one and let the other one ride?"

—JOHN SEBASTIAN

The Beggar and J. P. Morgan

Everyone wants goodies. I know I do. Sometimes a well-meaning community service in the city can become just that—a dispenser of goodies. When a group gives out things over time, people begin to depend on it. I remember hearing a story a long time ago about J. P. Morgan. I can't verify its truthfulness, but it is interesting nonetheless. The story goes that every day J. P. Morgan would pass a beggar on the street and give him a dime. At one point, Morgan had to be gone from his home for two weeks. When Morgan returned and passed the beggar again, the beggar was furious. "You owe me $1.40!" the beggar shouted.

The truth of the matter is that goodies may run out in life, but choices don't. That is why the person who turns devotion upside down and finds himself or herself serving in a community may need to help people make choices. When we think about the big picture, we know that the poor often feel as though they have no choices. The systems that assist them may make them feel dehumanized. In their mind, there seem to be no options, and they are depending on someone else to make decisions.

Because a person who is pressed down may feel as though there are no choices, I always try to help them see that they can make a choice. I might say, "I cannot give you any money, but we can offer you a meal tonight, and if you are really hungry, there is a church ten blocks away that is offering food right now." For me, that approach seems like such a better way to communicate, rather than saying, "No, we never give money." Part of my goal is to help people learn to make better choices.

When I was young, I tended to judge other people by the one area I thought I was smart in; therefore I thought I was smarter than a lot of other people. Now I know that there are all kinds of "smart," and different people around me possess different kinds of intelligence. One important kind of intelligence, I think, is the ability to make good life decisions. Some people seem to be better at this kind of intelligence than others.

All of us make abysmal life choices sometimes, but from the perspective of good sense, some people seem to make consistently the most destructive kind of choices. Paul says that "God gave us a spirit not of fear but of power and love and"—then there is this special word in Greek, that can mean "good sense" (2 Timothy 1:7). That last quality is sometimes what I pray for, both for myself and for those I work with—a spirit of "good sense" to make good choices given the circumstances.

Choices are powerful. As we read in the first few pages of the Bible, choices can bring greater freedom, or result in fear and guilt. The choices we make and consequences that come from them can't help but make us think about our place in the larger realm of life, about the cosmos, about God. Proverbs tells us that "when a man's folly brings his way to ruin, his heart rages against the LORD" (19:3). When things don't go well, we may blame ourselves, or our family, or the system, or deep down we blame God.

When a person sees that an essential part of our worship to God is service to those who are pressed down, the discussion of choices becomes quite emotional. We cannot coerce someone to make good choices, though I have tried. To see someone make poor choices is for me sometimes like watching someone hit themselves in the skull with a hammer repeatedly. They don't see how destructive their behavior is. Through the years, I have facilitated many memorial services where the people died because of the stupid choices they made. This seems to be the way of life. "Sooner or later everyone sits down to a banquet of consequences," Robert Louis Stevenson once said.

Often when we are involved in service, we may have to walk alongside someone who we know is making very wrong choices. Jesus realizes this when He tells the story of the prodigal son. The son demands his inheritance before the father dies, and the father gives it to him. The father loves the son enough not to coerce him to be something different, even though he knows the son's choice is destructive. I have thought many times about how the father felt as he watched his younger son going down the road, knowing how dangerous and destructive a path the son has chosen. But the father still let him go.

Why More Curses than Blessings?

*W*e don't have to get in a discussion of the sovereignty of God to know that we are confronted with choices. In the end, of course God who holds time and space in His pocket, who is the source of all things, who has given us every molecule of our being and brain and existence, rules over all we do. Still, in the Bible, in this smaller arena of perception, we are offered choices. "'See, I have set before you today life and good, death and evil. If you obey the commandments. . . . But if your heart turns away . . . Therefore choose life'" (Deuteronomy 30:15, 16, 17, 19). In the same speech (chap. 28), Moses tells us there are blessings if we obey the voice of the Lord, and there are curses if we will not obey the voice of the Lord. I have always been interested that there are 14 verses concerning the blessings of the Lord and 54 verses describing the curses. But now that ratio makes more sense to me. When we stop obeying the voice of God, problems compound on problems, things get worse and worse in unexpected ways just when we thought we had found a shortcut to the goodies. Life gets more and more complicated.

In any event, in the Book of Deuteronomy, life and death are set before us, and we are clearly told to choose life. The rest of the story of the people of God, including our own story, makes this gracious offer seem all the more bittersweet. Jesus comes and presents the people with a choice too. In the

Gospel of Mark, He starts His ministry by saying, "'The time is fulfilled, and the kingdom of God is at hand; repent and believe in the gospel'" (1:15). To repent means to turn around, to change our mind. This language of calling us to a choice seems so strong. Sometimes we have made a multiple series of wrong choices, so that complication piles on complication. Then we feel as though we could never come back to God. But we often say at Graffiti that no matter how far you have gone down the wrong road, it is the right road when you turn around. Therefore, we are never really very far away from God, no matter what we have done and no matter how destructive we have been. God is always there, right at our shoulder, when we turn around.

So just as Jesus shows us, the one involved with service can't just give things to people, no matter how important those things may be—food and clothing and shelter and even good advice. The servant of God is involved in helping the person in need make choices. We are involved in empowering them, regardless of their situation. I often have to say no to someone who has requested or demanded something they think I have. However, I try to help them see what choices they may have at that time.

Dealing with the Temper Tantrum Mentality

$\mathscr{F}$ather Alfred Boeddeker was for many years a famous person in the San Francisco area, known for helping the poor on a broad basis. Even though he died almost 20 years ago, his work still continues in a variety of ways in the Bay Area. In the dining area of the ministry in the Tenderloin district of San Francisco, they have two quotes on the wall. One of the quotes says, "The great activity of our life is to love." The other quote says, "I see God as one act—just loving, like the sun always shining." When I was younger, I worked with the vast array of community ministries there. By that time, Father Alfred was already 80 years old, so when he came to speak to us it was a special occasion. In Father Alfred's office, he had four words printed on his wall in huge letters—"Visualize, Organize, Deputize, Supervise." However, when he spoke to us, he didn't talk about a community service strategy. Instead, he always talked about how everything flows from the love of God. You and I are instruments, like a pen in the hand of the love of God.

Father Alfred said that we often work to win the battle and by doing so we lose the war. We triumph in getting the community room painted the color we want, but we lose the war because we alienated the participants by doing so. He said that showing kindness to others was the core of God's love. However, experience has shown us that such kindness does not mean always giving people what they ask.

I remember Father Alfred as the one who told us how to respond to those requesting help, by quoting a Benedictine saying. He said, "Sweet in the manner, firm in the thing." Whether the source is correct, I have used this saying many times and have often written about it. The saying helps me know how to be both kind and firm when giving people choices. Most people are so grateful to have someone help them. Some people, however, have learned that they can receive things by creating a scene, by shouting or cursing or refusing to cooperate. In a situation of great activity, some helpers will just give the person what they ask for to placate them. However, this approach to me does not take the person seriously, but only helps them continue in a tantrum mentality. This is the time to be both kind and firm, and let a person know what their choices are. Thank you, Father Alfred.

Community ministry workers are often aware of an uncanny sixth sense that those who are highly addicted or mentally ill (or both) sometimes have. It is an ability to discern your area of vulnerability. They sometimes seem to pinpoint an area of guilt in your own life in order to gain what they want, or play on an area of question in your life where you are uncertain. This ability is not surprising, since using this skill has probably helped them survive. Nevertheless, it is important to be aware of spiritual forces beyond us, both good and evil ones. These forces sometimes seem very present in these situations. It is important to develop the ability to say no to someone who is addicted and who knows how to manipulate a person's feelings.

Mental illness on the streets is one of the saddest things I see. Sometimes the choices of the mentally ill seem so limited. One English intellectual, who for many years was the main support for his mentally ill mother, said it most succinctly in summary. "Every trouble in life," he said, "is a joke compared to mental illness." With other homeless people we work with, there seems to be some element of choice, whether they are runaways or unemployed or addicted. But in my books, the mentally ill carry the heaviest burdens.

Giving people choices doesn't mean being harsh. I have quoted in earlier books a saying that has been attributed to philosophers thousands of years ago: "Be kind, for everyone you meet is fighting a hard battle." We never totally understand the background of a person, any person, even the people closest to us. Kindness may be the only thing we can offer. As we do more community ministry, one of the greatest temptations for me is to categorize people. I will think, *Oh, I have heard this story so many times before*, or *This person is bipolar*, and then I stop really listening. In a sense, to categorize someone means putting them in a box and ceasing to see the real possibilities. We feel wrongly that we have heard it all before. We haven't.

But being kind doesn't mean we have to agree to everything the person is asking for. I've noticed that people can accept a lot of noes if the person giving those negatives has truly listened to them. It is the impatient and abrupt no that makes us feel less than human. Sometimes people want to have their story heard even more than they want their request granted.

Common Sense That Has Helped

*A*s we help people sort out choices, some rules are obvious. In talking to people, we hold to the "rule of three," whether we are with children or youth or adults. Three people should always be in the same area all the time, for everyone's protection. Even in personal counseling, we have a glass door with others outside; and if that is not possible, we have an open door with someone working in the next room. We have said before that we work to have men working with men and women working with women. Finally, if a visit is required, we always go two by two. These simple rules help us to avoid obvious problems. Good sense helps us be in a context that offers healthy choices. On the street, we can always make foolish choices and walk into unwise situations. We remind our workers of the words of Jesus — "Be . . . wise as serpents, and harmless as doves" (Matthew 10:16 KJV).

We want to walk along with a person, regardless of his or her age, and help him or her make good choices, to have that holy good sense which will help that person thrive in life. When I first began working in the storefront at Graffiti, we had a group of teenagers that blew my mind. They were rowdy, rebellious, and violent, and opportunities to work together turned out to be opportunities to show how tough they were. Still, they kept coming. My co-workers and I were falling apart. We didn't know what to do with this group. A professor at Teachers College, Columbia University, helped us try to sort things out. She came and did some workshops for us. The workshops were a revelation for me. When I described an incident of rebellion in the group, she helped me think about things in a different way. One of the things I carried away from her teaching involved how I looked at the teenagers.

As I remember, she said at one point that the goal for us is not really to get these teenagers to do what we wanted them to do. The goal is to help them learn to make good choices. When a leader said we were going to do something and a teenager resisted, we could simply say, "Well, I can't force you to do anything." This, in fact, was very true. Some of these teenagers were bigger and stronger than me and the other leaders. We could continue, "Now, you have a choice. You can either do what the group is planning to do, or you can leave. It is your choice." Somehow, this approach helped us see things in a different light. Either choice they made was respected.

The games we played involved giving different teenagers a leadership role in their group and we had a system of rewards. In the end, the teenage leader decided how to give the members of his group the rewards. These violent young men got better and better at making good leadership choices. The whole approach was a revelation to me. The burden of keeping a group of rowdy teenagers in line shifted. I had choices too, and I could always say what was happening wasn't pleasant for me so we might quit early. Granted, we had the luxury of being an optional program (not like school), but we could interact together to learn to make good choices—I was modeling appropriate choices and they began to do the same for each other.

I was able to carry on some of these things I learned when I became a parent of my own teenagers. This process of growing up is a process where my sons got more and more freedom to make choices. I told them at 12 years old that the next 6 years would be a process of their having more and more freedom. Sometimes the freedom would not come as quickly as they wanted it to. Sometimes the boundaries would seem unfair to them, but the boundaries would keep expanding. I told them that even in those difficult times, I still loved them.

We learned together that both the parent and the teenagers have options. At one very short time in both my sons' lives as teenagers, this saying helped me: "If you are rude to the supplier, you don't get the supplies." It may sound harsh, but our journey together was learning that both the son and the parent have options, and we were learning together to make better choices.

One of our children's directors used to have a saying as we discussed issues with the parents and other adults. She would say, "Some children are bigger than others." To be honest, if adults have the equivalent of a temper tantrum, they don't get the supplies either. We have the responsibility to be both sweet in the manner and firm in the thing. Perhaps one of the greatest gifts God has given us is the ability to make choices. When we see service to others as a part of our worship, when we really get involved in people's messy lives, we find that we are all on this road together. Each moment we are all making an array of choices in the vast web of circumstances around us, and each choice has consequences.

principle #10
It's About Kingdom, Not Castles

"'The kingdom of heaven is like a grain of mustard seed that a man took and sowed in his field. It is the smallest of all seeds, but when it was grown it is larger than all the garden plants and becomes a tree, so that the birds of the air come and make nests in its branches'" (MATTHEW 13:31–32, JESUS).

"The chief difference between words and deeds is that words are always intended for men for their approbation, but deeds can be done only for God."

—LEO TOLSTOY

The Vastness of a Mustard Seed

A man in our city has been an encourager and mentor for our second and third Graffiti sites. I love to talk to him. He grew up in the Bronx and has served on our national denominational level, at one point helping review loans and guarantees that the denomination was able to provide. From there, he has encouraged planting churches in our city. He has talked to a lot of different churches and he has a unique perspective. This is something I have carried away from our talks—my friend will remind me, "It's about a kingdom, not castles." A castle is a fortress, built to impress and at times to keep people out. A kingdom is vast and extensive, hopefully with no walls for barricades. Sometimes we have poured our energy into building a noteworthy castle, but forgot that we are to be about a kingdom.

Jesus is quite clear about God's kingdom in the Lord's Prayer. He uses the speech tempo of the time—parallelism. Parallelism states the same thing a second time, often expanding on the meaning of the original line. Think of Jesus' prayer—"Thy kingdom come, thy will be done." First Jesus prays that God's kingdom comes. Then He explains what this kingdom is like. It is a place where God's will is done, just as it is in heaven. If we think about it, this is a huge, expansive explanation, beyond our petty understandings of church or Christian groups. Any place that does God's will becomes part of His kingdom.

One of the most surprising things to me about the Bible is its vastness. Even when God gets extremely particular, He often includes some long-term, vast promise. Even when God chooses someone, He often chooses the person so that the person can include others in an expanding circle.

God makes a very specific call to Abraham. God tells Abraham that He will bless him, but the offer of blessing extends to everyone in the world. God ends the blessing by saying, "And in you all the families of the earth shall be blessed" (Genesis 12:1–3). We begin to see that part of the promise to Abraham fulfilled in Jesus. We mentioned before that Jesus starts His ministry by saying, "The kingdom of God is at hand; repent and believe in the gospel" (Mark 1:15). Jesus compares this kingdom to a mustard seed, a very small seed (Mark 4:30–31). Ancient gardeners knew that the mustard seed can grow and take over the whole garden. It is hard to keep it confined. This was Jesus' sense about the kingdom, that it was ever-expanding and taking over. Jesus did envision a barricaded castle with gates, but that castle was hell, not heaven. Jesus saw hell as a fortress with a closed gate and walls, walls not built to keep people in, but to keep God's kingdom out. He sees the church as a mobile force kicking in the doors of that staid, stable fortress of hell—"I will build my church, and the gates of hell shall not prevail against it" (Matthew 16:18).

For Jesus, this kingdom is a multiethnic, transglobal enterprise. He instructs the 11 disciples, who are located in a specific culture in a little Roman colony, to "make disciples of all nations" (Matthew 28:19). The vastness of the vision of these first-century documents is stunning. Paul carries this same vision on, telling the inquisitive Athenians that God has "determined allotted periods and the boundaries" of *every* nation, "that they should seek God" (Acts 17:26–27). This is not a national God, but a God who is transnational. John of Patmos has a vision where it is clear that the work of Jesus is not for one group of people, but that Jesus has "ransomed people for God from every tribe and language and people and nation" (Revelation 5:9). It sounds repetitive because it so important: every tribe/language/people/nation. This is big.

For me, the Bible keeps exploding my little ethnocentric, geographic perceptions. Tennyson has a wonderful couple of lines:

> *Our little systems have their day;*
> *They have their day and cease to be:*
> *They are but broken lights of thee,*
> *And thou, O Lord, art more than they.*

That is what I see. Our little systems, our little programs, our little conceptions, our little castles crashing down under the vastness of God and His intentions.

Paul says that he takes "every thought captive to obey Christ" (2 Corinthians 10:5). The story of Christ continues to sink deeper into our hearts. For me, almost every story becomes the story of Christ. Now almost every book I read and every movie I see seems to proclaim it, from *The Great Gatsby* to *Batman*. The heart of these stories is almost invariably the story of someone sacrificing for someone else. For me, the kingdom seems to be taking over like mustard seed.

Promoting Smallness on a Large Scale

This mobile, active, unrestrained kingdom starts to influence, wherever it goes. Jesus shows us the way. When we read about Him, leprosy isn't contagious, healing is. Uncleanness isn't contagious, wholeness is. Jesus didn't hesitate to touch the lepers or the dead. He ruined every funeral He went to. His kingdom was on the move. He never asked someone to come to the synagogue or to church. Never. He went to where the people were, and said that the kingdom of God was right there.

We can't really see how big this kingdom is. We can only see little parts of it. In the Bible, people often have very little sense of what God is doing. Abraham is a great example, a nomad who traveled around three or four millennia ago. As he took steps of obedience as a servant, did he really understand all that would follow? Did he understand about Moses and David and Jesus and us? Did he know that eventually half the world looks to him as father? Could he visualize the churches and synagogues and mosques all over the world, more numerous than the stars in the sky? Could someone really evaluate what had happened through Abraham a hundred years after his death? A thousand years? Can we really evaluate the results yet today? Where would Christian believers be if Abraham had said something different to God? He could have said, "No, thanks, God, I think I will stay here where I am with my family. It is more comfortable."

If we are to turn worship upside down and inside out and focus on service, we have to let go of our own little castle. It's not about money for our program, or our ideas, or our ministry, or our talents. Things are much vaster than that. Our mission church in the Lower East Side sees the lessons of faith we learned as we built a building in Manhattan. That building will pass away, yet the stories of people whose lives are changed will go on forever. All the buildings in Manhattan will pass away. The city itself will not last forever either. Our nation will not last forever. Most of the things we put our time into can become castles, stone and mortar that will pass away. God has plans of His own to accomplish the kingdom. Our part is to be obedient in the tiny little place He has put us, regardless of the bigness or the smallness of the particular "castle" we are working on.

Recently I listened to a CD lecture by a popular Christian author speaking at a church. He said something I had never thought of. He said that Ecclesiastes speaks about a time to build up and a time to break down (Ecclesiastes 3:1–8). He said that God may put you in a place where He is using you to build up. But perhaps, perhaps, He is letting you be a part of something breaking down. This thought, that God might put someone into something to help it diminish, was revolutionary to me. I keep seeing that God is bigger than my little preconceptions. Who knows what God's assignment might be for us? I am resting in God's promise, that He will speak to us and tell us whether to turn to the right or to the left (Isaiah 30:21).

When we begin to think about kingdom rather than castles, smallness and bigness take on an entirely new perspective. Some Graffiti missions work has taken on the motto, "Promoting smallness on large scale." We do not know if doing the smallest, most personal thing may in the end be the most important thing. If we only think about the biggest castles, we may miss the kingdom, which may be working like a mustard seed in the garden.

We are familiar with tipping points in business. Those are the times some small merchandise item becomes the rage and takes over the nation. But there are tipping points in Christ too. According to scholars, Paul's little groups in Corinth and Thessalonica and Ephesus were relatively small. There were a lot of other important things going on in these vast urban centers. An impartial observer at the time might have missed altogether these small meetings that were happening, these small meetings that would have such great impact centuries later. That's just the way things are. Human experience is too rich and complex and intricate for us to evaluate realistically what is happening. In this ocean of data, we sometimes just have to trust and keep obeying.

I Can Plod

Sometimes the upside-down servant will have a very difficult time evaluating his or her own success. We are tempted to look for the castles and miss the kingdom, the kingdom working in small ways, in a little boy's lunch before the crowd of thousands, in the mustard seed, in the lost coin, in the 1 lost sheep as opposed to the 99, in all the stories in the Bible that turn our grand conceptions inside out. Sometimes we just have to keep plugging away.

William Carey, the missionary to India, had to deal with a number of battles as he worked on translations of the Bible into the languages of India. He had to deal with mission disputes, denominational disputes, mental illness in his wife, conflicts between the young missionaries and the older missionaries, and on and on. I love the statement he made at one point— "I can plod." My wife wants to have a stained-glass window made for a church with that simple statement on it. Sometimes, as upside-down servants, when we can't see the castles, we can only say, "I can plod."

On the other hand, sometimes the castles we build take on too much importance. Leo Tolstoy, the Russian writer, wrote a wonderful short story about getting caught up in the castle of our own goodness, called "Father Sergius." In the story, a soldier converts to become a monk. Eventually his heart for God becomes well known and people come and revere him because of his goodness. He continues in his holy works and rejects the compliments of the people, but secretly he enjoys them and eventually builds his own sense of identity around what they think. He falls into an evident sin, which ironically helps him realize how unrighteous he really is. The monk runs away and feels as though God tells him to visit a cousin he knew in childhood. The other children used to laugh at her for her clumsiness and dullness.

In his visit to his cousin, he sees that she serves her family and is unrecognized. The world would see the life of his cousin as a dismal failure. Yet through her unrecognized service, he sees what serving others really is. Father Sergius has this insight and realizes, "I lived for people, pretending it was for God, while she lives for God and thinks she is living for people. Yes, one good deed, one cup of water given without thought of reward is worth more than all the benefits I ever worked for men." His vision of his own little castle of human praise was crumbling. The last scene in the story shows him being treated contemptuously by some superficial tourists who don't know who he is, thinking he is a wandering homeless person with little significance. They give him a little bit of money, which he accepts and secretly gives to a blind beggar who needs it more. He is joyful at last.

At the end of Tolstoy's life, people from all over the world were coming to him as he sought to follow in a simple way the tenets of Jesus. At this phase of his life, he said that the biggest temptation of a man was not sexual lust. The biggest temptation of a man was the lust for fame. Clearly the short story he wrote was a working out of his own inner journey, as people lauded Tolstoy more and more for his goodness. In his own way, he realized he was using God against God, using the Sermon on the Mount to build his own little castle of reputation.

Our own generation has had to deal with two biblical truths that must be placed side by side. One truth is that God loves us and wants to bless us. If we read Deuteronomy 28, we know that God knows what a blessing is—health, finances, a good reputation, abundance. Jesus, too, knows what a blessing is. He never tells people they need to keep that sickness because it will teach them something. He always works toward healing. He never tells a crowd that they just need to learn to eat less, and they will learn from their hunger. He always gives them more than enough food. He is the Good Shepherd. A good shepherd doesn't have scraggly, sickly, emaciated sheep.

On the other hand we are called to take up the Cross. The Cross did not just mean pain. It meant shame. It meant the sign of failure in a society. It meant walking a way of sorrow. It meant the crowds would not understand. It meant a bad reputation. The upside-down servant may face loss rather than expansion. As Martin Luther wrote in his song, "Let goods and kindred go, this mortal life also, / The body they may kill." The truth of God's blessing and the truth of God's challenge must be laid side by side. Both God's blessing and God's challenge are in the Word of God. To only emphasize one over the other is to move toward something other than Christ's way.

If we only focus on our own castles, we may not understand when our castle melts away as the kingdom moves ahead. By their nature, castles are built and through time fall into ruins. Even the strongest castles crumble eventually. But this deep kingdom goes on forever.

conclusion
The Two Hands of Christ — Release Work and Relief Work

"Now you are the body of Christ and individually members of it" (1 CORINTHIANS 12:27, PAUL).

"Christ has no body now on earth but yours, no hands, no feet but yours. Yours are the eyes with which he looks compassion on this world. Yours are the feet with which he walks to do go good; yours are the hands, with which he blesses all the world."

—TERESA OF ÁVILA

Fat Cows Overlooking the Needy

*W*e said it at the beginning. God finds our worship hateful. At least that is what the Bible says. God says He has had enough of our offerings (Isaiah 1:11). He finds our appointed times of worship hateful and a bore (1:14). He will not listen to our prayers unless we learn to do good, seek justice, and correct oppression (1:15–17). If we ignore His instruction, we are in a sad state.

God portrays us as sleek, overfed cows, offering something every morning and tithing every three days, yet we are oppressing the poor and crushing the needy. Still, our biggest concern is that our spouses bring us the right kind of drink (Amos 4:1–5). These are not my words—they are the words from the prophets.

Jesus says the same thing. He portrays a group of people who revere the Word of God and argue over the finest points of how to tithe correctly. Yet their very preoccupation has made them forget the real matters of justice and mercy and loyalty (Matthew 23:23–24). He describes us as people who have gotten everything out of whack, straining at a gnat and swallowing something bigger than a horse.

The church saw the same thing. James the brother of Jesus saw church services where the people honored the rich person who entered, forgetting that this rich person was involved with oppressing the poor and dragging the needy into litigation

(James 2:1–7). James describes the one who is warped in his or her devotion to God, telling the poor, "God bless you!" but never giving any real food or clothing (vv. 14–17). This is a sad state. When we read these words, they should make us squirm.

This doesn't really undermine the fact that we are saved by grace. Some people think that James's words are a critique on Paul's emphasis on faith. James's words are a critique, but they are a critique of a false faith, a false devotion, a "pseudo-Paulinism," so to speak. If we read the entire set of the letters of Paul, we see that for Paul, faith is the total response of the total person to a total relationship with Jesus the Christ. Faith for Paul is not some little word game, where someone says a prayer asking Christ into his or her life and then proceeds on with life in the exact same way as he or she did before, with a few religious activities added. For me, if we read Paul's letters and James's letter, they may use different words but they say the same thing. And what they both say is a challenge.

We have mentioned before a sentiment Søren Kierkegaard said a long time ago. He implied that taking part in hypocritical public worship is treating God as a fool. If God is God, the logic of Kierkegaard's statement is compelling. The challenge to a walk with Christ is real, and we better not try to play around with it.

In review, *devotion* means feeling or displaying strong attachment or affection. The original Latin words mean "derived from a vow." It is a serious loyalty and a merging of our whole being into something larger and better than ourselves alone. As poet and preacher John Donne mentioned long ago, we're not really islands, we are all connected in a deep way we cannot even describe. Trying to portray ourselves as islands, responsible only for ourselves is an illusion. Serving others puts us back into balance, and reminds us that we are not self-contained. These tangible actions may seem extreme to some, but when we listen to our remarkable God, they begin to make sense.

We Are His Hands

ecause we are connected, Paul describes us, when we ally ourselves with Christ, as being the body of Christ (e.g., 1 Corinthians 12). We are all different, but related. When the earthly Christ was here, He brought not only the words of life, but bread and healing. The physical earthly Christ is not here anymore. He has appointed us to be his body; we are His hands.

A long time ago, I read about a man doing church and community work in San Francisco. He said that the church always reaches out with the two hands of Christ in ministry. One of the hands is relief work, and one of the hands is release work.

This image gave me a way to understand things. Relief work was the immediate response to need. When disaster strikes a life, the first things needed are things that bring relief, no questions asked—food, clothing, shelter, survival training. There will be time to fill out forms later. These are the acts of immediate generosity that I see all the time. I have watched a Christian in brutally cold weather simply take off his own gloves and give them to a man who was cold. I have seen a Christian exchange shoes with a homeless man during a snowstorm. Relief work is the simple act of giving someone a sandwich, no questions asked. Relief work hands a cold person a coat, or gives them a mattress to sleep on. The church, the body of Christ, will always do some of this. The poor instinctively know this. In times of difficulty in the city, the poor don't line up in front of the agnostic society. All over the city, they flock to the church for help. If we eliminate this part of ministry, as some well-meaning Christians want to do, we become callous and hard-hearted to real need, thinking that we can only work on training others to stand on their own.

The other hand of Christ, however, is release work. Release work is involved in setting people free from bondage. By the act of Christ, release work sets people free, regardless of who they are, from the stupid prison of sin. Release work also helps set people free from destructive habits, addictions, defeating behaviors, and stinking thinking. Release work often has an immediate component, and a component that takes much longer. In the Bible, the liberation from Egypt is a prime example. As we have said before, it took God one day to get the people of God out of Egypt. It took God 40 years to get Egypt out of the people of God. Release work often takes a retreading of the brain and a transformation of the way we look at things. We encounter setbacks and restarts on the road to release. We may experience substantial release but not total release. Sometimes we may have what one Christian called "muffled victory." This is victory that is triumphant but not total. If a church ignores release work, and only does relief work, it becomes a church that is patronizing. Ultimately a church that does only relief work may just become another part of the person's codependence, another self-justifying crutch for the person to continue in addiction and sin.

So true devotion doesn't mean going to a gathering to sing the best and latest Christian songs and hear the most interesting preacher, as good as these things may be. The "conference mentality" can deceive us into thinking we are devoted when we are not. As we can see in the Bible, it has happened many times before, using many different trappings and a variety of bells and whistles. True devotion means being something, being the body of Christ, and acting out the heart of God, being "do-voted" rather than just "de-voted." True devotion goes back to the root word from *devotion*. It relates to the vow with God, to be the hands of Christ, working in release work as well as relief work.

Such an intention does not mean becoming a legalist, someone measuring everyone else in a new kind of works-righteousness. It does not mean getting into another evaluation list, monitoring ourselves in terms of how many justice issues we are involved with. Martin Luther and the other reformers delighted in the Scriptures 500 years ago. What a joy to see again that we are justified by faith alone. As we mentioned in the introduction, the new Bible teachers of that time would sometimes compare faith to a flame and works to heat. No one would try to create heat without a flame. It doesn't make sense. We only have to give attention to the flame, and the heat will come. However, if there is not heat, you have to ask the question whether there is a fire. Let us start again and truly respond to God in faith, not just raise our hands in worship service. Responding to God in faith is the fire. The heat of actions will come.

I have the privilege from time to time to go hiking in the mountains. It is a big deal for me. Since I live in a tenement apartment on a street full of buildings in Manhattan, just seeing trees and grass is pretty exciting. I love to hike to the little mountain streams. Some of them look as though they come right out of the rocks in the mountain. When things have been very dry, some of the little streams dry up. The vegetation around them gets dry and brittle. The path next to them gets dusty. But when the rains come, it may take just a little poking with a stick to open up the mouth of the stream. The stream, from some vast resource that I cannot see or understand, begins to bring life to everything around it again. Trees thrive, animals come to drink. It is time to let the rains come, and to poke around at the mouth of the stream again. It's time.

There are a thousand ways to say this. Ethics has always been such an important part of our faith. Jesus wouldn't let us get away with anything else. In Matthew, He portrays the last judgment as an evaluation of whether we did the right thing for the hungry and thirsty and naked and homeless and sick (25:31–46). We don't have to manufacture this part of our faith. It is in the core of God's Word. Just as in the time of Amos or Isaiah, worship is still irrelevant to God without these actions. To paraphrase Jesus' story, the "church planter" and the "church helper" who pass by the hurt man still missed the point.

Knowing Christ can never be simply a mystical experience contained in itself. No matter how sophisticated our teaching tools and praise music become, it is not enough. Martin of Tours is a good example of that. He grew up in a military family a very long time ago—in the fourth century. He was drawn to Christianity as a young person, even though Christianity was not part of his family and not part of the military culture at the time.

Martin became a soldier, and through that experience, confirmed his commitment to Christ. One story tells of his returning home in the winter. With his heart for the Lord, he had given practically all his clothing away to help others stay warm, everything but his military cloak. As he walked down the street of the city, he encountered a homeless man who was freezing. He didn't have anything else to give. He hesitated. Finally he took his sword and cut his military cloak in half to give the freezing man something. As Martin continued on the city street, people laughed at him for looking ridiculous, being almost naked with just half of a cloak. But some were perhaps a bit ashamed in their laughter, because they could have clothed the homeless man without having to reduce themselves to nakedness.

That night, Martin had a deep experience of devotion. When he was asleep, wonder of all wonders, Christ the King of kings and Lord of lords appeared to him in a dream.

Christ was wearing half a cloak.

appendix a
Gallery of the "Do-voted"
(That's pronounced as the word *do* and
not as the word *doe*.)

*The root word of devotion can mean "related to a vow" (de+
votus). We are the devoted in our loyalty to God in the context
of a vow. Somehow this word devoted has deteriorated to the
expressing of just the trappings of the vow. We need a new word.
To regain the sense of action for those who are "de-voted," I am
calling those who are in balance the ones who are learning to do
good. They are the "do-voted."*

*I did not list every single person cited in this book in the "Gallery of the
'Do-voted.'" I only listed those who I felt had particular insights to offer
in further reading. Some of the people listed below are people with very
different views from my own. A few might not claim to be a Christian.
However, each of them made a connection with something in the book.
If I didn't include someone about whom I wrote, I often listed the source
of information within the book itself.*

Amos—He was definitely "do-voted." As an eighth-century BC prophet, he saw a world bustling with extravagance and religious activity. The whole book is a discourse on the difference between fake worship and what we need to be doing. He is graphic in describing the women as sleek cows who oppress the poor and ask their husbands for something else to drink (4:1). He describes the businesspeople as trampling the needy and just waiting for the Sabbath to be over so that they can start taking advantage of people again (8:4–6). I talk about Amos in the introduction and conclusion.

Alfred Boeddeker—He was a recent Franciscan friar who helped start many programs for the marginalized in the San Francisco area. He taught me and many others how to be firm with someone in need and kind at the same time. He is discussed in chapter 9, concerning giving choices.

Dietrich Bonhoeffer—Bonhoeffer reflected deeply on the meaning of grace and the true cost of discipleship. This is a quote from his book *The Cost of Discipleship*: "Cheap grace is grace without discipleship, grace without the cross, grace without Jesus Christ." I mention him in the introduction as a reflection on the difference in doing and just saying.

David Brainerd—He is an eighteenth-century American missionary who is an example of someone who didn't give up after repeated failure. Expelled from Yale, his first few attempts at ministry seemed to be a failure. Something special happened as he worked with Native Americans in New Jersey, and many accepted Christ. Still, he died at 29 years of age, and his influence could only be measured after centuries. We refer to him as one who didn't have big numbers in chapter 2. His *Diary* is a classic.

William Carey—This English Baptist missionary in the early nineteenth century was remarkable in his diligence to work to share the gospel. He is an example of someone who keeps plugging away for the kingdom, not just for a castle. I quote his famous phrase, "I can plod," in chapter 10.

Charles Dickens—Dickens was the nineteenth-century English writer who portrayed so well characters that acted in kindness and also characters who only talked piously about kindness. We mention him in chapter 2 in discussing the difficulty of evaluating success.

Francis of Assisi—He was mentioned in chapter 6 because he seemed so good at doing one thing at a time. When God told him to rebuild the church, he went begging for stones and literally rebuilt one small church. He helped those who had the least. He wasn't much of a talking head.

Abraham Joshua Heschel—The books of this twentieth-century rabbi are worth reading. I keep going back to things he said as he reflected on the Bible. His book *The Prophets* is wonderful. He quotes extensively on the places where the prophets say we must look out for the oppressed. His sections on the anger of God are particularly revealing to me (see chap. 7). His thoughts on the Bible help us get started in the introduction.

Isaiah—Jesus likes to quote this prophet, who spoke hundreds of years before Jesus' birth. He is one of the primary prophets who retools our understanding of what worship is. I quote him extensively in the introduction and also in several other chapters.

Jesus—He is the one who gave us the Sermon on the Mount. All we have to do is read it to understand how important it is to be "do-voted." His grace and resurrection empower us to do.

Job—Job lost ten children in one day and asks a lot of questions. Eventually God tells him to gird up his loins like a man and God asks Job 77 questions of His own. It makes one stop and think. We talk about Job when we talk about toughening our hearts in chapter 4.

Søren Kierkegaard—Because the nineteenth-century Danish philosopher had such a sharp eye for the hypocrite in worship, I wanted to quote more fully his strong words that are referred to in the conclusion from *This Must Be Said—So Let It Be Said*:

This has to be said; So Let It Be Said. *Whoever you are, whatever in other respects your life may be, my friend, by ceasing to take part (if ordinarily you do) in the public worship of God, as it now is (with the claim that it is the Christianity of the New Testament), you have constantly one guilt the less, and that a great one: you do not take part in treating God as a fool by calling that the Christianity of the New Testament, which is not the Christianity of the New Testament.* . . . The official worship of God . . . is, Christianly, a counterfeit, a forgery (p. 73).

Martin Luther—Luther's radical emphasis on justification by faith never mitigated the act of doing. For example, here is a quote from his sermons when he returned to Wittenberg after some had misunderstood what he had said: "God does not want hearers and repeaters of words [James 1:22], but followers and doers, and this occurs in faith through love. For faith without love is not enough—rather it is not faith at all, but a counterfeit of faith, just as a face seen in a mirror is not a real face, but merely the reflection of a face [1 Corinthians 13:12]." I talk about Luther's understanding of faith and works in the introduction and the conclusion. A helpful book for me on Luther was *Luther the Reformer: The Story of the Man and His Career* by James M. Kittelson.

Martin of Tours—Martin was born to a veteran Roman officer in what is now Hungary in AD 316. Eventually he became bishop of Tours in what is now France. I first read the story of Martin's cloak in *Classics of Christian Missions* by Francis M. DuBose. I mention the story in the conclusion.

Micah—Micah is an eighth-century BC prophet who gets it. He challenges the leaders who easily cry out to the Lord, but God will not hear them because of their oppression of their own people (3:1–4). He castigates the priests who "teach for a price" (3:11). I refer to him in the introduction.

Don Miller—The favorite book that I have ever read by Don Miller is *To Own a Dragon: Reflections on Growing Up Without a Father*. It was so helpful as we deal with a society of people who often have no father present. I reference one of his examples in the introduction.

Albert Schweitzer—There is so much I disagree with when I read Schweitzer, but for me, he always brings something to the table. He refused to be a talking head, but spent his life in service in Africa. I picked up *The Mysticism of Paul the Apostle* at a used bookshop somewhere. I was shocked at how thoughtful and relevant it was, even though it was written in 1930. As I mention in the introduction, Schweitzer was deeply concerned about summarizing Paul with the concept of justification by faith alone. He felt that we lost the "doing" (my interpretation of his words) that is so inherent in Paul if we only use this concept to read his writings. I mention him in the introduction in discussing worship and service, grace and law.

J. R. R. Tolkien—Tolkien for me has the greatest insight in the little quiet things that affect our lives more than the great leaders and warriors. The hobbits in his writings are such great examples of how their little actions affect the much wider paths of our lives. I refer to him in chapter 1 in discussing the delusion of the dramatic.

Leo Tolstoy—This nineteenth-century Russian writer struggled with a sense of his own privilege and how his life matched with the Sermon on the Mount. You can't help but respect his honesty about it. I mention the remarkable story "Father Sergius" in chapter 10. Even our own sense of our goodness can become a little castle.

John Wesley—I mention Wesley in chapter 5, because he understands the inside work of God. This eighteenth-century preacher speaks a lot about grace, but he is very concerned to be "do-voted." The following is an example of his practical instructions:

"Do you not know that God entrusted you with that money (all above what buys necessities for your families) to feed the hungry, to clothe the naked, to help the stranger, the widow, the fatherless; and, indeed, as far as it will go, to relieve the wants of all mankind? How can you, how dare you, defraud the Lord, by applying it to any other purpose?"

John Woolman—This eighteenth-century Quaker, abolitionist, and itinerant preacher acted out the gospel so that people could see it in his lifestyle. He refused to wear dyed clothes or sell molasses or rum because these things were involved in the slave trade. He refused to ride in stagecoaches because of the cruelty to the horses. He was probably considered an oddball in his own time, but he was "do-voted." Eventually, trusting the Spirit, he was able to help lead Quakers to give up slavery much earlier than most of America. His book *The Journal of John Woolman* is inspiring, though a bit tedious. It has never been out of print since it was published. I mention him in chapter 3.

Brother Yun—This Chinese evangelist understands that things are an "inside job." He recounts great outward difficulties in his book *The Heavenly Man*, but he refuses to let them make him bitter. We talk about him in chapter 5.

appendix b

My Short List of Community Ministry Rules

(These are my rules to myself, that I have developed over 30 years.)

"For we are not, like so many, peddlers of God's word, but as people of sincerity, as commissioned by God, in the sight of God we speak in Christ" (2 CORINTHIANS 2:17, PAUL).

Vision Rules

1. The bigger the city, the more personal we need to become (see chap. 2).
2. "Relief work" is necessary, but work toward "release work." Move from dispensing things to training (see conclusion).
3. God is not a God of coercion. We do not *require* people to hear the gospel in order to get "stuff." However, we always *offer* an option to hear the good news (see chap. 2).
4. Speak well over the smallest gifts. Respect your partners (see chap. 5).
5. Work for the kingdom, not for castles (see chap. 10).
6. Be light, not lightning (see chap. 1).

Working with Others' Rules

1. Be sweet in the manner, firm in the thing (see chap. 9).
2. Instead of saying no, give people choices (see chap. 9).
3. Don't position yourself so that you are working harder than the person in need (see chap. 8).
4. Do not do things for someone else that they could and should do for themselves (see chap. 8).
5. You are responsible to keep a person from sabotaging a group or program. You cannot escape being the authority figure (see chap. 7).
6. When stopping an altercation, choose the saner person, tell them your first name, and ask for their first name. Then, using their first name, respectfully ask them to speak with you outside or in a removed place (see chap. 7).
7. When dispensing relief material with a large number of people present, mercy can be crueler than justice (see chap. 7).
8. Never disagree with a co-worker publicly. Address the issue privately and quickly (see chap. 7).
9. People who have severe addictions or mental illness often have very high skills in discerning your vulnerability. These skills are how they survive. Learn when to say no to someone with addictions (see chap. 9).
10. Continue to provide services, not money (see chap. 8).
11. Aim to have men work with men and women work with women (see chap. 8).

12. Always work toward the "rule of three"—three people present in any ministry situation. Even in private counseling, have a glass door or an open door with a third person in the other room (see chap. 9).

13. When you are on the street, be as wise as a serpent and as gentle as a dove. Don't go into foolish situations (see chap. 9).

14. Go two by two. Don't go into new places or apartments alone (see chap. 9).

15. Resist the urge to categorize people. Don't assume you know their story (see chap. 9).

16. When being an advocate for someone, keep a record of every phone call and inform the official of these previous phone calls. Don't give up simply because someone doesn't return calls (see chap. 4).

17. It is often more important to hear a person's story than to grant their request (see chap. 9).

18. For most people, attention is the big payoff. Do not reward temper tantrums in children or adults (see chap. 7).

19. Help people learn to bury their failures, not frame them (see chap. 5).

20. Be kind, for everyone you meet is fighting a hard battle (see chap. 9).

21. Everything is a joke compared to mental illness (see chap. 9).

Self-Care Rules

1. Take a day off each week. This rule is one of the "big ten" in the Bible (see chap. 6).

2. Find a forum with co-workers to vent about professional frustrations in ministry (see chap. 7).

3. As an adult, it is not right to have at-risk youth or children fill your personal needs for healthy relationships. Associate with peers on your day off (see chap. 6).

4. Plan your prayertime in the morning and refuse to take engagements at that time. If you don't plan your day, someone else will do it for you (see chap. 6).

5. When someone demands that you do something on your day off, simply tell them you have a previous commitment (see chap. 6).

6. Cultivate a little self-deprecating humor, you pompous windbag (see chap. 7).

Graffiti Community Ministry

Graffiti Community Ministry started in a storefront almost 40 years ago. Now it works to express God's love in tangible ways for thousands each year. It has also started Graffiti 2 in the South Bronx, Graffiti 3 in Brooklyn, and Gotta Serve in Long Island, as well as fostering and supporting almost 30 new churches while acting as mother church, aunt church, or grandmother church. It partners with a number of other ministries in New York City in a commitment to do the small thing to serve the unserved. For more information, contact Graffiti Community Ministry at 205 East 7th Street, New York, NY 10009, (212) 473-0044, or go to graffitichurch.org.

New Hope® Publishers is a division of WMU®, an international organization that challenges Christian believers to understand and be radically involved in God's mission. For more information about WMU, go to wmu.com. More information about New Hope books may be found at NewHopeDigital.com. New Hope books may be purchased at your local bookstore.

Use the QR reader on your
smartphone to visit us online at
NewHopeDigital.com

If you've been blessed by this book, we would like to hear your story.
The publisher and author welcome your comments and
suggestions at: newhopereader@wmu.org.

Resources for
Upside Down Living!

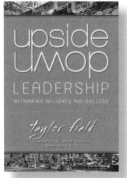

Upside-Down Leadership
Rethinking Influence and Success
TAYLOR FIELD
ISBN-13: 978-1-59669-342-5
N124147 $14.99

Upside-Down Freedom
Inverted Principles for Christian Living
TAYLOR FIELD
ISBN-13: 978-159669-376-0
N134117 $14.99

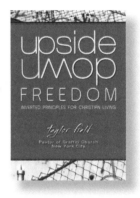

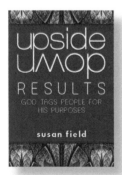

Upside-Down Results
God Tags People for His Purposes
SUSAN FIELD
ISBN-13: 978-1-59669-404-0
N144110 $14.99

Available in bookstores everywhere.
For information about these books or our authors visit NewHopeDigital.com.
Experience sample chapters, podcasts, author interviews, and more.

Download the New Hope app for your iPad, iPhone, or Android!

NEW HOPE
PUBLISHERS
Gospel-Centered. Missions-Driven.